Legal Almanac Series No. 26

PUBLIC OFFICIALS:
ELECTED
AND
APPOINTED

by **HUGH Y. BERNARD**
A.B., B.S. in L.S., J.D.
Of the District of Columbia Bar

1968
OCEANA PUBLICATIONS. INC.
DOBBS FERRY, NEW YORK

© Copyright 1968 by Oceana Publications, Inc.
Library of Congress Catalog Card Number 68-54014
Oceana Book No. 1-26

Manufactured in the United States of America

TABLE OF CONTENTS

Chapter 5

Chapter 6

Chapter 7

Chapter 8

ABOUT THE AUTHOR

Hugh Yancey Bernard was born in 1919 in Athens, Georgia. He is a graduate of the University of Georgia (A. B., 1941), Columbia University School of Library Service (B. S. in L. S., 1947) and the George Washington University Law School (J. D., 1961). He is a veteran of World War II, having served in the Army Air Forces, with overseas duty in the Philippines. For 13 years Mr. Bernard was employed in the Library of Congress, during 12 of which he served in the Copyright Office. As a law student, he served on the staff of the **George Washington Law Review**. Since 1960 **Mr. Bernard** has been Librarian of the Law Library at The George Washington University, and since 1968 holds the rank of Associate Professor of Law. He is admitted to the bar of the United States District Court and the United States Court of Appeals of the District of Columbia Circuit. Professor Bernard is the author of **The Law of Death and Disposal of the Dead** (1966; Legal Almanac Series no. 57).

PREFACE

This little book is directed to the interested reader who desires information about the law governing public officers and the governmental process. It may prove useful as enrichment or supplemental reading for college classes in political science, for more advanced social studies classes in high schools, and in adult education classes. Lawyers, perhaps, may find it helpful in refreshing their memories of the law concerning public office in its relation to the administrative process. If it helps to make citizens more informed about this area of the law, it will have served its purpose.

The author expresses his gratitude to the authors of the materials listed in the bibliography. These sources have proved most helpful to him. He assumes full responsibility for any errors, however, and asks that readers call his attention to any they notice. This will prove helpful in preparing later revisions of this book.

Hugh Y. Bernard
Law Librarian
The National Law Center
George Washington University
Washington,D.C.

March, 1968

Chapter 1

FROM TORCHLIGHT TO TELEVISION

Public Office in America

A few postage stamps at the rural or neighborhood post office.

A few packets of seeds from the Congressman.

Within the memory of many persons now living the above two items virtually comprised the average citizen's total contact with his Federal government. Unless he served in the armed forces, traveled abroad and needed a passport, imported goods and paid the tariff duty or ran for public office at the national level, he had almost no other direct contact with Federal authority. True, a businessman who was forced to go through bankruptcy, an inventor or author who desired patent or copyright protection, persons homesteading land on the public domain in the West and those concerned with navigable waters and certain forms of interstate commerce might have dealings with Federal officialdom. These were very much in the minority, however. The citizen paid no direct tax to his Uncle Sam. Except for brief periods during the Civil War and during the early 1890's there was no Federal income tax until 1913, and for the average wage earner it was not until the eve of World War II that he had to file a return and pay any actual income tax.

In those now vanished times, Mr. Average American lived out his life having only spasmodic dealings with officialdom at any level. Government simply played a minor role in his life and that of his family. Business and agriculture were only slightly regulated, and no arm of government intruded upon his decisions and planning concerning his retirement, savings, banking, investing, conditions of work, industrial or occupational safety, and care for himself or his loved ones in sickness or old age (except to the limited and humiliating

1

degree comprehended by the county alms house or poor farm). Common carriers (meaning almost solely the railroads) were regulated to a degree; a few rudimentary health regulations existed (mainly of the quarantine or pesthouse variety); a few licenses (marriage, dog, hunting and fishing) might be required at appropriate times; some form of public schooling was provided (although in the rural areas, and particularly in the Deep South, public schooling above the basic elementary level was almost nonexistent until well into the Twentieth Century). In cities and large towns, there was police and fire protection; streets were provided and maintained; the more progressive places had public libraries; there were parks in most larger communities; and following 1900 it came to be expected that the citizen should accept and be willing to pay for a larger group of public services of many kinds. The local tax collector was not far away, of course, and exacted his limited demands at regular intervals, although in many communities a citizen could discharge almost his total tax obligation by putting in a few days of work on the roads. Male citizens voted and served occasionally on juries. The county sheriff's aid was invoked in the service of process in some private lawsuit or in the levying of execution after judgment, and he was of course available for duty as a peace officer should the situation require it. The foregoing contacts just about sum up the total experience with government in its working aspects that the average rural or small town citizen was to know until little more than a half century ago. City dwellers knew but little more of government involvement in their lives.

Nevertheless, the citizen did feel deeply concerning his government. Elections and campaigns livened up an otherwise dreary round of toil, relieved in the rural and small town areas only by the coming of the circus or some traveling theatrical troupe. The citizen of that day found in the excitement of the torchlight parades, barbecues, clambakes, debates and oratorical contests, and other blatant manifestations of political activity the flattering sense that he was regarded as important, his vote counted for something, and that he was a person of consequence after all. In the cities of the East, where the immigrant tide poured in from Europe, political machines grew up and, although denounced as corrupt (which no doubt they were by turn-of-the-century or modern standards), they served a valuable social and economic purpose. In an age when direct and formal welfare services were not provided at any governmental level, it does not seem today so monstrous that a machine politician should have traded a load of coal or an order for groceries to a poor family in exchange for the votes of its male members on Election Day. In many places, no public relief program existed otherwise; and private charity, particularly during the recurring financial and business "panics" of the times, could not carry the load.

As population swelled, as people moved from farm and hamlet to city, as cities burgeoned to megalopolitan proportions, as agriculture and ranching gave way to industry and industry in turn to the service-oriented occupations, as self-reliance and self-sufficiency gave way to interdependence, and as life in short became too complicated and involved for any person to meet his own needs entirely by his own efforts, the relationship of the citizen to his governments (local, state and national) inevitably and inexorably changed. The social and economic history of the United States during the present century, and that of its states, counties and local entities, to a great extent records the steady demands placed by the citizenry upon government, and government's efforts to meet those demands. Beginning with the passage of acts regulating the civil service and interstate commerce in the 1880's, and an anti-trust measure in the early nineties, Congress began to regulate more areas of hitherto private or local concern. These laws were followed, after 1900, by a wave of statutes in the fields of conservation and reclamation, food and drug regulation, banking and financial control, farm and forest and natural resource management, labor regulation and protection, workmen's compensation, vocational education, health and sanitation, labor organization and collective bargaining, social security, and a wide range

3

of welfare and relief measures—with these and many other devices, government entered the life of the average citizen.

For better or worse, we live in a government-involved nation. Government, of course, is people, and many of these people are public officials. Since they perform some of the acts of sovereignty that inhere in government, they are themselves governed by law and by legal principles. To give some indication to the average citizen of his legal relationship to the sovereign, as that sovereign is represented by the human agents who carry out its services and exercise its powers, is the aim of this little book. The citizen should know something of how public office, both of the elected and appointed variety, is obtained and held (and lost), how the law governs the acts of public officials, the nature of the powers they exercise and the limitations on those powers, and the influences (both legal and extra-legal) that bear on the setting of and changing of policy. He should know the ways by which the citizen may bring his influence to bear on public officialdom, so that government may be and seem less like a bloated and impersonal Frankenstein's monster and more like what it should be—the means by which the people's collective civic demands are channelled and controlled to provide such services for the citizen as can best be provided collectively rather than individually. The wheels of power are not without brakes, reduction gears and governors. An informed citizenry, fully aware of its relation to the government and to the human instrumentalities of that government, is the best assurance that governmental power will be kept in bounds and directed toward wholesome, popularly approved goals.

What Public Office Is and Is Not

In the broadest sense, of course, every person who draws his compensation from the public treasury at any level for performing any duty for the sovereign or subordinate public power that employs him is a "public official." Thus, a postal clerk at the registry desk, teacher, policeman on the beat, member of the President's Cabinet, Internal Revenue agent, statistician in the Agriculture Department, librarian, judge, army officer, city councilman, deputy sheriff or forest ranger —each may at some time and for some purpose be considered a "public official." However, in legal thinking, "public office" may be said to vest only when certain requisite elements coalesce in a single position at a single time. These elements are well summed up in a Federal court decision which expresses clearly the requirements: "Giving the word 'office' the sovereignty of the state attaches for its technical qualities, five elements would seem indispensable in order to make a public office of a civil nature. (1) It must be created by the Constitution or the Legislature or by a municipality or other body with authority conferred by the Legislature. (2) There must be a delegation of a portion of the sovereign powers of government to be exercised for the benefit of the public. (3) The powers conferred and the duties to be discharged must be defined either directly or indirectly by the Legislature or through legislative authority. (4) The duties must be performed independently and without control of a superior power other than the law. (5) The office must have some permanency and continuity and the officer must take an official oath." **Pope v. Commissioner**, 138 F.2d 1006 (1943).

In order to define what is meant by "a portion of the sovereign powers of government," the Missouri Supreme Court has used the following terminology:

> If specific statutory and independent duties are imposed upon an appointee in relation to the exercise of the police powers of the State, if the appointee is invested with independent power in the disposition of public property or with power to incur financial obligations upon the part of the county or state, if he is empowered to act in those multitudinous cases involving business or political dealings between individuals and the public, wherein the latter must necessarily act through an official agency, then such functions are a part of the sovereignty of the state." **State ex rel. Pickett v. Truman**, 333 Mo. 1018, 64 S.W.2d 105 (1943).

5

Repeatedly, in the decided cases involving questions turning on whether a given position is or was a "public office" or whether a given incumbent was a "public officer," the courts have stressed the necessity that the occupant of the position, to qualify as such, must have performed or been empowered to perform some part or portion of the sovereign power of the jurisdiction that put him in office. At certain times and for certain purposes, the same person in the same office may be considered a "public official" and at other times and in other contexts he may not. In general, it may be safely said that occupants of seats in legislative bodies, even at the local municipal level, are public officials; judges and judicial officers are public officials in almost every instance (about the only exceptions might be at the lowest level, where a committing magistrate, for example, might in certain cases have actually no judicial discretion to exercise. In other cases the same magistrate might exercise true judicial, and therefore, sovereign powers.) A local justice of the peace and ex-officio notary public would be a public official when presiding over his justice court, but would not be when notarizing a document. The degree and presence of supervision by other officials or employees is important. A judge, even though subject to judicial review by higher courts should his decisions be appealed, is nonetheless a public official. His decisions are arrived at through construing the law, as he is given to understand it through the constitutional and statutory principles, rules and the decided cases touching on the question before him; not by taking counsel of the appellate bench which may some day pass upon the accuracy of his interpretation. Likewise, there is precedent for holding that a tax assessor or higher tax administrative official is a public official; the executive officer (mayor, city manager, etc.) of a city is such an official; the higher municipal, state and county officers, Federal officials in the Cabinet and sub-Cabinet levels, the occupants of regulatory and quasi-judicial bodies, and usually all those whose appointments are subject to Senate confirmation are considered public officials. For the purpose of this book, however, the term "public official" will be limited to civilian positions at any level of government, above the lower and middle levels of the career civil service, and excluding military officers, diplomatic and consular officials, the career foreign service, and quasi-military bodies such as the commissioned officers of the Public Health Service and similar persons. This is done to keep the work in bounds and because the average citizen has little or no formal contact with those categories of officials.

Chapter 2

HOW PUBLIC OFFICE IS ACQUIRED—
ELECTION

Voting and Election Laws

Constitutional and statutory controls govern the method of registering voters and determining their eligibility, conducting campaigns, holding elections and primaries, counting the ballots and recording and announcing the results of voting. Provisions exist for settling disputes, holding recounts or canvasses of the ballot, certifying candidates as winners and otherwise regulating the electoral process. These provisions of law, local, state and national, are treated in detail in another unit of the Legal Almanac series (No. 24, **Voting and Election Laws**, by C. E. Smith) and for that reason are not dealt with in any detail here. However, peripheral to the principal laws concerning elections and voting are many other legal matters that must concern the aspirant to public office and the interested citizen as he ponders the political scene.

The Political Party, Its Role

Although not mentioned at all in the United States Constitution, and mentioned in but few of the state constitutions, the political party nonetheless plays a vital and usually decisive part in the process by which public office is obtained and held in the United States at all levels. Even in the now-dwindling "one-party" jurisdictions, political party machinery is brought into play by means of conventions, petitions and primaries to nominate candidates for office. In such jurisdictions, "personal politics" and intra-party factional contests dominate the political process, since the nominee of the dominant party is virtually assured election, in what is often a cut-and-dried "general election." The political party evolved because all but the smallest areas and communities require a means by which the voters of similar interests and philosophical or economic approaches to government may make their collective wishes and concerns felt. Even where social and economic or other differences barely exist at all, the party continues in its necessary role in the political process because certain vested interests come to grow up in and around it—organizational machinery, patronage, personal loyalties, tradition and the need for a nexus that is difficult to define —a mystique perhaps, centering in persons and history and visceral feelings more than in concrete issues and principles. Suffice it to say that parties are inherently a part of the American political picture, and a grasp of the legal principles governing them is necessary for the aspirant to office and for anyone concerned about the office-obtaining process.

Obtaining this information is difficult, since it is usually not gleaned from a study of statute or constitution, nor in many cases from the decided court cases. News media tell part, but often not all, that is needed. The person must contact the party officials in his community, county or state. Dates for holding primaries or conventions, qualification rules by which one becomes a candidate for nomination, time deadlines required for announcing or declaring candidacy, fees to be paid (and when and to whom to pay them), petitions if any to be filed, how many signatures are required for them if needed (and the qualifications for signers), how one advertises or announces his entry into the primary campaign—these and many more matters are largely governed by the parties themselves through an apparatus of committees at several levels, chairmen and other officials. One aspiring to run under a party banner or symbol ignores the requirements to his peril, since if disqualified as a party candidate he would have to abandon his effort, or run in the general election as an independent, and possibly as a write-in candidate, with the handicaps that such status imposes.

One thing to be borne in mind is that, although the parties in the different states, counties and local entities have the same general names (Democratic, Republican, Liberal, Farmer-Labor and the like), they are actually autonomous, or nearly autonomous, bodies in the different jurisdictions. Each makes its own rules and conducts its own business, so far as its internal affairs are concerned, largely free of national or other unified control. At the time of the quadrennial Presidential campaigns, of course, most of them subordinate their separate concerns in the common effort to capture or hold the national government. Even then, however, a degree of independence exists that makes campaigning in one jurisdiction under a given party symbol a wholly different process from running in a nearby area under the same emblem. In most areas, party support for a candidate is predicated on a showing of party loyalty, a willingness to perform chores for the common cause, and even to support nominated candidates toward whom the fledgling aspirant may not feel personally or philosophically or ideologically drawn, in elections and campaigns antedating the magic one in which he casts his own hat into the ring. Generalizations are well nigh impossible to make, since in some areas a high degree of independence, ticket splitting and partyline jumping is tolerated and accepted; in others any deviation from the strictest loyalty to party chieftain, machine and nominees would make the would-be candidate a pariah, bereft of all hope of support from the organization. A "feel" for the party practice and tradition in the community itself is required. No book can teach this.

So far as state or local law is concerned, a political party is merely a group of qualified electors who represent a given percentage of the total voting population, and who file or submit petitions to permit themselves to organize as a party under a chosen name and designation for the purpose of entering candidates in elections for office. Once organized and sanctioned as a party, the group is protected in the use of its name against those who would confuse the electorate by organizing similarly-named groups. Some form of symbol, banner or emblem is often used on ballots and campaign material, and displayed in voting machines, to designate the position of names of party-endorsed candidates. These devices are protected by state law against wrongful appropriation by others, by means of laws similar to those at the national level protecting the "service marks" of non-political philanthropic and social service organizations. Sometimes at the state level petitions must contain not just an aggregate number of qualified voters but a distribution of them in different geographical locations or districts within the state.

State law usually sets up the party committees and provides for the holding of conventions, but leaves the details and procedures to the party organizations. In the eyes of the law and before the courts, these bodies are private voluntary associations. However, their processes are so clothed with a public interest that they may not be allowed to operate untrammelled. For example, when a private group called the Jaybird Democratic Club, in Texas, sought to define its membership (and eligibility to vote in its primaries or conventions) so as to exclude Negroes, the Supreme Court of the United States voided its action. The group was private, but it was performing a public function in participating in the effective selection of public officeholders and as such could not limit its membership along racial lines. **Terry** vs. **Adams**. 345 U.S. 461 (1953).

The state party committee, governing or holding the state convention, prescribes the general party organization for the state as a whole, draws up a constitution, rules or by-laws and periodically a platform for the state organization, and also endorses or selects candidates for statewide public office. It plays varying roles, in different states, in the control of local or district committees, caucuses or conventions and names a national committeeman and committeewoman from the state. In the Presidential election years, it selects the delegates to the party's national convention. The state convention chooses the party's Presidential electors, for appearance on the general election ballot in November. Interested persons should inquire into the widely varying local or district rules governing the choosing of convention delegates or caucus participants at those levels. Depending on whether one is concerned with state senators, delegates or representatives in the legislature, with judges or with county or local officials, there will be some form of local, district, circuit, county, city, town or ward meeting, convention, primary or caucus

11

to choose candidates and set up party organization for the applicable campaign.

The Campaigner on the Hustings

If the candidate receives the nomination or endorsement of his party, or if he is regularly entered as a candidate in the primary, the ways in which legal considerations and requirements impinge on him multiply greatly. Several of the most important are enumerated or described herein. For example, every state except Rhode Island, Delaware and Nevada has enacted some form of corrupt practices act, limiting or controlling campaign expenditures and contributions for elections. Even in the named states, various Federal statutes must be consulted and complied with. States having such acts vary widely, from very few restrictions (Alaska, Illinois, Louisiana) to strict limitations (Maryland, New Hampshire). More important than the wording of the statute, however, is the degree of enforcement and the interpretations placed by courts and enforcement officials on clauses and limitations that are included. The chart here included summarizes the limitations by state.

LIMITS ON CAMPAIGN FUND-RAISING AND EXPENDITURE, BY STATES

ALABAMA. Applies to primaries and general elections for Statewide office, Senators and Representatives. Statements of campaign receipts and disbursements required of candidates, but not of parties. Statement required within 15 days after a primary and within 30 days after a general election. Contributions by corporations prohibited, but not by unions. Restrictions on type of expenditure, and on total expenditure by candidate (but not on amount spent in behalf of candidate).

ALASKA. Applies to primary and general elections, statewide offices and Senators and Representatives. No statements required of candidates or parties. No effective limitation on fund raising or expenditure; no reports or statements required.

ARIZONA. Applies to primaries and general elections, statewide office and to Congress races (in primaries only). After election, statements of receipts and disbursements required of candidates and parties (no time deadline). Corporate (but not union) contributions prohibited. Expenditures limited at primaries except for advertising, stationery and printing, and certain travel-related costs. No restriction on character of expenditure.

ARKANSAS. Primaries and general elections; statewide and for Congress. Candidate (but not party) must report expenditures, but not receipts. A corrupt practice pledge is taken before, and candidate expense is reported after, election. Limitation on total expenditure by candidate, exclusive of travel and hotel expense.

CALIFORNIA. Primaries and general elections; statewide and for Congress. Statements (after election) required of candidates and parties, showing receipts and disbursements. No time deadline. No prohibition on gifts by corporations or unions. No elective candidate for state office where licenses are issued may solicit or receive gifts from a licensee. No limit on total expenditure by or on behalf of candidate, but character of expense is limited.

COLORADO. Primaries and general elections; special elections to fill Congress vacancies. Statewide office and Congress. Within 10 days after primary or 30 days after general or special election, statements are required from parties and candidates, showing receipts and disbursements. No prohibition on corporate or union gifts, no limit on character of expenditure nor on total amount spent by or on behalf of candidate.

CONNECTICUT. Primary and general elections; statewide and for Congress. After election, statements required of receipts and disbursements by candidates and parties. No time limit. Contributions by corporations prohibited, but not by unions. No one may give under assumed name. Total expenditure by candidate limited; on behalf of candidate, no limit if sums are spent by independent political committee.

DELAWARE. No effective corrupt practices legislation.

FLORIDA. Primary and general elections; statewide and

for Congress. Statements of receipts and expenditures required of parties and candidates, to be filed before and after elections. Corporate, but not union, contributions prohibited. No one person may give more than $1,000; no gifts may be received from persons holding horse or dog racing permits, those selling intoxicants, and public utilities regulated or franchised by the state (nor from their officers, partners or directors). Character of expenditures limited, but no limit on amount spent by or on behalf of a candidate.

GEORGIA. Primaries and general elections; statewide and for Congress. No statements required of parties or candidates, regarding receipts and expenditures. Contributions by corporations prohibited. No other restrictions.

HAWAII. Primaries and general elections; statewide offices and for Congress. Campaign receipts by parties and candidates need not be reported; disbursements must be reported by candidate and by agent or committee of party acting on behalf of candidate. Statement required within 20 days. No restriction on corporate or union giving, but character of expenditure is restricted. No limit on totals spent by or on behalf of candidates.

IDAHO. Primaries only are governed; statewide offices and for Congress. Candidate must file statement of disbursements (but not receipts) within 20 days after election. No prohibition on corporate or union giving. Restriction on character of expenditure; total primary expenditures by candidate are limited, but no limit on sums spent on his behalf.

ILLINOIS. No general corrupt practices law; contributions may not be received from insurance corporations; no other limitations.

INDIANA. Applies to primaries and general elections; statewide and for Congress. Statements (within 45 days after election) must be filed by candidates and parties showing receipts and disbursements. Corporate and union contributions prohibited. Restrictions on character of expenditure, and on total amounts spent by or on behalf of candidate.

IOWA. Applies to primaries and general elections, statewide and for Congress. Candidates must file statements of receipts and disbursements within 30 days after election;

parties, within 30 days after general elections only. Corporate contributions forbidden; union contribution forbidden only if union is incorporated. Gifts may not be received from nonresident persons, firms or corporations. Total spent by candidate is limited, but not sums spent in his behalf.

KANSAS. Applies to primaries and general elections; statewide office only. After election (no time limit) candidates and parties must file statements of receipts and expenditures. Corporate giving prohibited, but not union giving. Total amount spent by candidate limited, but not amounts spent in his behalf. Character of expenditure is controlled.

KENTUCKY. Primaries and general elections; statewide and for Congress. Candidates, but not parties, must file statements of receipts and disbursements, 15 days before and 30 days after election. Union contributions not prohibited, but no candidate may receive gifts from corporations or from those with whom candidate must deal in his official capacity. Total expenditures by or on behalf of candidate are limited; also character of expenditures.

LOUISIANA. Primaries and general election, statewide and for Congress. No statements required of parties or candidates. Corporate contributions forbidden; also gifts from a wide range of state and local civil servants and officials. No other restrictions.

MAINE. Primaries and general elections for statewide office only. Parties and candidates must file statements of receipts and disbursements between 10 and 25 days before election; final report within 30 days afterward. No restriction on corporate or union giving; character of expenditures, but not the amount, is controlled.

MARYLAND. Primaries and general elections; statewide and for Congress. Within 20 days after election, parties and candidates must file statements of receipts and disbursements. Corporate giving prohibited, but not gifts from unions. Limit of $2,500 contribution from any one source not a candidate. Character and amount of expense is limited, but a wide range of candidates' advertising, mailing, telephone and other costs are exempted from the limit.

MASSACHUSETTS. Primaries and general elections, statewide and for Congress. Statements required of candidates and parties, showing receipts and expenditures, within 14 days after primary; second Tuesday before general election and within 14 days after such election. Unions may give, but corporations and public officers and employees may not. Character, but not amount, of expense is limited.

MICHIGAN. Primaries and general elections; statewide and for Congress. After election but before certification to office, candidates and parties must file statements of receipts and expenditures. Corporate, but not union, giving is forbidden. Restrictions on character and total amounts of expenditures for and by candidates.

MINNESOTA. Primaries and general elections, statewide and for Congress. Within eight days before and 10 days following primaries and general elections, parties and candidates must file receipt-expenditure statements. Corporate, but not union, giving prohibited. Restrictions on character and total amount of expenditures by or for candidates.

MISSISSIPPI. Applies to statewide and Congressional primaries only. Candidates, but not parties, must file statements of receipts and expenditures the first and 15th day of each month of the campaign. No restriction on corporate or union giving, nor on character of expenditures. Total sums spent by or for candidate are limited.

MISSOURI. Primaries and general elections; statewide and for Congress. Campaign receipts and disbursements by parties (and disbursements only by candidates) must be reported within 30 days after election. Corporate, but not union, giving prohibited. Amount spent by, but not for, candidate is limited.

MONTANA. Primaries and general elections; statewide and for Congress. Receipts and disbursements by candidates must be reported within 10 days after election; by parties, within 15 days after election. Corporate, but not union, giving prohibited. No limit on sums spent in behalf of candidate, but sums spent by him and by his relatives and "associates" is limited.

NEBRASKA. Primaries and general elections; statewide

and for Congress. Receipts and disbursements by parties, and disbursements only by candidates, must be reported "after election." Contributions by corporations and incorporated unions prohibited. Character, but not total amount, of expenditure is limited.

NEVADA. No corrupt practices act.

NEW HAMPSHIRE. Applies to primaries other than Presidential preference and delegate primaries, and to general elections. Statewide and for Congress. Two receipt-disbursement statements required of parties and candidates, six days before and 10 days after, the election. Corporate and union contributions are forbidden; also gifts from partnerships or state classified employees, anonymous or concealed gifts, disguised loans, and gifts over $5,000 except by candidate himself. Character of gifts is limited, also (with certain exemptions) total sums spent by or for the candidate.

NEW JERSEY. Primaries and general elections; statewide and for Congress. The Friday or Saturday before, and 20 days after, the election, both parties and candidates must file reports of receipts and disbursements. Public utilities, banks and insurance companies may not make contributions; unions and other corporations are not restricted. The character and total amount of expenditure by candidate is limited, but not sums spent for a candidate.

NEW MEXICO. Primaries and general elections; statewide and for Congress. Candidates, within 10 days after election; and parties within 30 days after, must file reports of receipts and disbursements. No prohibition on corporate or union giving, but no political party money may be spent on behalf of a primary candidate. Sums spent by candidate (except for personal expenses) are limited in amount; no limit on sums spent on his behalf.

NEW YORK. Primaries and general elections; statewide and for Congress. Before and after elections (no time limit) both parties and candidates must report their receipts and disbursements. Union giving not prohibited, but corporate gifts and gifts by owners of polling places are barred. Limits on total sums spent by or in behalf of candidates.

NORTH CAROLINA. Before and after elections, all

17

candidates must report their receipts and expenditures; parties must report their receipts, but their disbursements only in general elections. Corporate, but not union, giving is forbidden. No other regulations.

NORTH DAKOTA. Primaries and general elections; statewide and for Congress. Fifteen days after elections candidates must report their disbursements, but not their receipts. No party reports required. Union giving not prohibited, but corporations and those giving under other than the donor's own name may not support candidates. Limits on character of expenses allowed, and on total amounts spent by or for candidates (exempting personal travel and certain printing costs).

OHIO. Primaries and general elections; statewide and for Congress. (Representatives only). By 4:00 p.m. the 45th day after election, both parties and candidates must file statements of receipts and expenditures. Corporate, but not union, giving is forbidden. Character of expenditure is controlled, and the total amount by the candidate; no limit on sums spent for a candidate.

OKLAHOMA. Primaries and general elections; statewide and for Congress. Within 15 days after election, candidates must report their disbursements; within 10 days after a general election, party campaign committees must report both receipts and disbursements. Corporate, but not union, giving is forbidden. Total sums spent by or for candidates are limited.

OREGON. Primaries and general elections; statewide and for Congress. Within 15 days after election, parties and candidates must report their receipts and disbursements. Certain corporations may not contribute; no prohibition on unions. Character of expenditures is controlled; total sum spent by candidate is limited to a percentage of the salary of the office sought; no limit on sums spent on candidate's behalf except by relatives and "associates."

PENNSYLVANIA. Primaries and general elections; statewide and for Congress. Within 30 days after any primary or election, both parties and candidates must submit statements of receipts and disbursements. Both union and corporate giving is prohibited. Character, but not total amount, of expenditures by and for candidates is limited.

PUERTO RICO. Quarterly, within 30 days after end of quarter, both candidates and parties must report their receipts and expenditures. Corporate giving is prohibited; also individual gifts in excess of $300 in an election year and $200 in other years; no ban on union gifts. An electoral fund exists against which parties may draw up to $75,000 annually ($150,000 in election years); sums so drawn may be used only for controlled purposes. No limits on sums spent by or for candidates.

RHODE ISLAND. No corrupt practices act; Federal law provisions govern.

SOUTH CAROLINA. Primaries and general elections; statewide and for Congress. Before elections, candidates must file statements of disbursements only; no requirement for party reports. No prohibition on corporate or union giving; no limit on total sums spent by or for candidates; restrictions exist concerning character of disbursements.

SOUTH DAKOTA. Primaries and general elections; statewide and for Congress. Within 30 days after elections, parties and candidates must report their receipts and disbursements. Corporate, but not union, giving prohibited. Character of expenditures controlled; limits on total sums spent by candidates (except for written or printed matter) and for candidates.

TENNESSEE. Primaries and general elections; statewide and for Congress. Campaign disbursements must be reported by parties. Candidates must report disbursements five to 10 days before election; their managers must report disbursements within 30 days afterwards. Corporate, but not union, giving prohibited. Character of expenses not controlled, but limits are placed on total sums spent by or for candidates.

TEXAS. Primaries and general elections; statewide and for Congress. Party reports not required; candidates must report receipts and expenditures before and after elections (no time limits). Both union and corporate contributions are forbidden. Character of expenditures is controlled; limit on sums spent for a candidate, but not on sums spent by him.

UTAH. Primaries and general elections; statewide and for Congress. Party and candidate reports required of receipts and disbursements, as follows: second Saturday after first disbursement; second Saturday each calendar month thereafter; also the Saturday before any primary or election. Corporate, but not union, giving forbidden. Character of expenditure is controlled, but no limit on amounts spent.

VERMONT. Primaries only; statewide and for Congress. Within 10 days after primary, candidates must report their disbursements only. No prohibition on corporate or union giving. Character of expenditures is not controlled, but total sums spent by or for candidates are limited.

VIRGINIA. Primaries and general elections; statewide and for Congress. Within 30 days after election, caucus, convention or primary, candidates must submit statement of disbursements. No prohibition on corporate or union giving; character of expenditures is controlled; also limit on total amount spent by the candidate.

WASHINGTON. Primaries only; statewide and (partisan primaries only) for Congress. After primary, candidates (but not parties) must submit report of receipts and expenditures. No prohibition on corporate or union giving. No other restrictions.

WEST VIRGINIA. Primaries and general elections; statewide and for Congress. Before and after elections (no time limit) parties and candidates must report their receipts and disbursements. Corporate, but not union, giving is prohibited. Limits on amount and character of disbursements by and on behalf of candidates.

WISCONSIN. Primaries and general elections; statewide and for Congress. By 5:00 p.m. on the Tuesday preceding an election, and on the Saturday following such an election, both parties and candidates must report their receipts and expenditures. No prohibition on union giving; corporations and co-operative associations may not contribute. Limit on character of disbursements, and on total sums spent by (but not for) candidate.

WYOMING. Primaries and general elections; statewide

and for Congress. Within 20 days after election, both parties and candidates must report their receipts and disbursements. Corporate, but not union, giving prohibited. Character of expenditures controlled; amount spent by a candidate (except travel expense) limited, also sums spent for him.

The technique of conducting the campaign, and the strategies and tactics to be employed, are in many ways governed by law. The candidate would be most unwise to run afoul of local ordinances governing such matters as the size, location and placement of campaign posters and placards, for example. Also, he distributes handbills according to local laws and requirements designed to prevent littering the streets. Door to door canvassing, possibly, is governed by various requirements in different localities. There are many provisions of state law designed to control political campaign advertising matter. Many of these laws make it mandatory that the name and the address of the originator of any printed campaign leaflet, poster or advertisement inserted in a newspaper or periodical be shown. Penalties are imposed for the anonymous circulation of campaign matter that would be in other ways unobjectionable. Massachusetts, for example, prohibits the circulation of unsigned political advertisements, posters, circulars or similar materials and forbids the circulation of publicity matter bearing names of endorsers without their authorization. Also, any advertisement inserted in a media publication must bear the names and addresses of two or more officers of the sponsoring group, or the name and address of the individual inserting the ad if it is not a group project. No false statements may be published in such material, designed either to aid or injure a candidate in his campaign. The word "advertisement" must be used above any material of this character printed in the news or editorial portions of a newspaper or periodical, if confusion with the regular columns of the medium would be likely.

The state of Massachusetts also regulates the use of the word "veteran" in political advertising, restricting it to lawful former members of the United States armed forces, or (with proper qualification) veterans of foreign forces.

It is a misdemeanor in many states to deface, injure, unlawfully remove or cover any political poster or sign during the campaign period. In Arizona, this prohibition is qualified to exempt from penalty the removal of such signs if they were placed on private property without permission or in public space in violation of ordinances or the like.

In several states (Massachusetts again is an example) it is forbidden to interfere with or obstruct or hinder the distribution or lawful posting of printed matter publicizing an election candidate or party. Florida, Kansas and other states have similar legislation. Florida forbids the publisher of a newspaper or the operator of a broadcasting station to charge any more to a political candidate for advertising than he would charge for equal commercial space or time. Kansas prohibits the bribing of a publisher or editor for his endorsement of a candidate, prohibits the payment by party or candidate for the cost of transporting voters to the polls, and makes it a misdemeanor to circulate any anonymous publication attacking a candidate.

The foregoing examples make it clear that the state's corrupt practices legislation must be checked carefully before embarking on a campaign. The annotated code of California alone, for example, includes two fat volumes devoted exclusively to election law; these statutes require no less than 30,202 "sections" as of late 1966 to cover all legislative pronouncements on the subject of local and statewide elections and political practices.

Besides the state laws, many local ordinances need to be checked. For example, in most populated places, some form of noise control and abatement regulation may prevent or restrict the use of sound trucks and public address systems in political campaigning; parades may require permits; use of public space such as parks may also require proper authorization, and the like. Despite the breadth of recent court decisions concerning freedom of speech and assembly, the political aspirant would be wise to conform as far as possible to reasonable local regulations, so long as they are impartially applied to all alike.

Care with legal and regulatory minutiae may well make the difference between a smooth running, effective, harmonious campaign and one afflicted with lost motion, extra expense, wheel-spinning and friction with authorities and governmental officials whom it would be tactically unwise to antagonize. Where principle is not involved, controversy should be reserved for bouts with one's opponents on the issues and not wasted and diffused in peripheral bitterness over trivia concerned only with the mechanics of the campaign.

Federal regulations also bear very significantly on the campaigner's progress toward Election Day. From minor postal regulations concerned with mailing charges for political fliers and circulars, to major matters like the Federal Communications Act's "equal time" provisions in regard to broadcasting, the Federal authority is concerned even with state and some local political contests.

Political Broadcasting:
"Fairness Doctrine" and "Equal Time"

An understanding of these requirements in regard to political broadcasting requires some review of the nature and background of broadcasting regulation. Unlike the press, which does not employ any element of the public domain and which has been "free" throughout our history since the Bill of Rights was written into our Constitution, the broadcaster or telecaster employs a limited number of frequencies in the airwaves. These are regarded as public property, to be used by publicly licensed firms for the benefit of the public. Since the passage of Federal laws regulating broadcasting, stations have been licensed to permit utilization of the airwaves for the public interest, convenience and necessity. For years the Federal Communications Commission and its predecessor, the Federal Radio Commission, forbade "editorializing" on the air, in the belief that these licensed monopolies should not espouse one doctrine, party or side in controversial issues to the detriment of opposing views. "The broadcaster cannot be an advocate," was the Commission's view prior to 1949. In that year, the Commission issued a report, entitled "Editorializing by Broadcast Licensees," in which it altered its regulations so as to permit the expression of political and other controversial views by stations. In order to control this expression on the air, the Commission evolved the "Fairness Doctrine," which may be summarized as follows:

(1) Licensees have an affirmative obligation to present fairly all sides of matters in controversy, and a duty to encourage the airing of all sides of important controversial issues over their facilities.

(2) Licensees cannot meet their obligation by refusing to broadcast opposing views when a demand is made on the station for broadcast time.

(3) An absolute standard of fairness cannot be prescribed; licensees will not be penalized for honest mistakes or errors in fairness, where their overall records show an effort to meet reasonable standards of fairness in the presentation of views and comments. What is demanded is "a duty to operate a radio (or television) station with good judgment and good faith guided by a reasonable regard for the interests of the community to be served."

From the political partisan's standpoint, it is important to know that, in the Commission's words from an actual case, ". . . where, as here, a station's editorials attack an individual by name, the 'fairness doctrine' requires that a copy of the specific editorial . . . shall be communicated to the person attacked, either prior to or at the time of the broadcast . . . so that a reasonable opportunity is afforded that person to reply." The "fairness doctrine" does not impose a requirement that in every case the same amount and quality of time be made available to the opponent or spokesman for an opposing view, but it does require that essential fairness in the particular case be observed. The Federal Communications Commission's weapon, to insure compliance, of course, is the refusal to renew the license of an offending station should demands for observance of this doctrine remain unheeded. The time to be afforded the opponent to rebut the expression of an earlier hostile editorial is to be "free" time of the nearest quality as practicable, to that used in the first instance. Needless to say, a rule of such breadth and (of necessity) such vagueness has given rise to much trouble, particularly in the heat of campaigns. Competent legal counsel would be indicated should the candidate run into cases where a hostile broadcasting station attacked him or his party or faction during a primary or election contest.

In addition to the "fairness doctrine," which is a matter of regulatory law promulgated by the F.C.C., there is the "equal time" requirement written by Congress into the Federal Communications Act as amended and appearing as Section 315 of that act. This requirement applies only to political candidates, whereas the "fairness doctrine" extends to all expressions of editorial opinion on disputed issues.

Section 315 of the Communications Act of 1934, as amended in 1959, reads as follows:

"(a) If any licensee shall permit any person who is a legally qualified candidate for any public office to use a broadcasting station, he shall afford equal opportunities to all other such candidates for that office in the use of such broadcasting station: **Provided**, that such licensee shall have no power of censorship over the material broadcast under the provisions of this section. No obligation is imposed upon any licensee to allow the use of its station by any such candidate. Appearance by a legally qualified candidate on any—

(1) bona fide newscast,

(2) bona fide news interview,

(3) bona fide news documentary (if the appearance of the candidate is incidental to the presentation of the subject or subjects covered by the news documentary), or

(4) on-the-spot coverage of bona fide news events (including but not limited to political conventions and activities incidental thereto),

shall not be deemed to be use of a broadcasting station within the meaning of this subsection. Nothing in the foregoing sentence shall be construed as relieving broadcasters, in connection with the presentation of newscasts, news interviews, news documentaries, and on-the-spot coverage of news events, from the obligation imposed upon them under this chapter to operate in the public interest and to afford reasonable opportunity for the discussion of conflicting views on issues of public importance.

(b) The charges made for the use of any broadcasting station for any of the purposes set forth in this section shall not exceed the charges made for comparable use of such station for other purposes.

(c) The Commission shall prescribe appropriate rules and regulations to carry out the provisions of this section."

If the time afforded one candidate by the station is "free" time, then under the terms of the act, "free" time of e-quivalent quality must be made available to opposing candidates. If the time made available to the first candidate is "paid" time, then equivalent "paid" time must be afforded to opposing candidates.

In practice, the workings of Section 315 have given rise to controversy, partly because some of the terms used in it have not been susceptible of ready definition. What is a "legally qualified" candidate? Does this include announced primary candidates, or is it limited to party nominees? Definitions of "bona fide," "newscast," "news documentary" and the like have proved elusive in certain contexts. Moreover, rulings of the F.C.C. in disputed situations, during campaigns, must be made quickly if they are to have any effect on the race being run by the candidates. Government regulatory bodies simply are not equipped to marshal the relevant facts and data, consider them in the light of the law and the precedents and come up with a just ruling in short order. That the record is not worse than it is is a tribute to the earnest efforts of the Commission to issue prompt rulings while they have some meaning.

One serious legal problem comes up during the quadrennial Presidential election years. The act, of course, does not distinguish between "major" and "minor" parties, nor could it do so and remain just to all voters and candidates. The result has been that some stations, being specifically not re-quired to take any political broadcasting, were refusing to accept any from the Democratic or Republican candidates lest they be confronted (as they have been) with demands from a host of minor "splinter" parties and candidates, some of them of the crackpot variety, for "equal time" with the major contenders. Thus, one of the Congressional

26

purposes in enacting the section was being frustrated. An object had been to provide a maximum of fair and full coverage of the Presidential campaigns for the enlightenment of the electorate. When stations refused to carry such broadcasting because of the minor party problem, the public was to that extent denied enlightenment and information on the major issues, candidates and parties. Beginning in 1960, Congress has enacted legislation suspending the operation of the section in Presidential years only, and only for the two chief offices.

Thus it was possible, for example, for the famous 1960 television debates between John F. Kennedy and Richard M. Nixon to take place without effective demands from splinter-party candidates to participate on equal terms. One can view the dilemma faced by Congress, the stations and the regulatory body with sympathy, and yet question whether a policy of denying coverage to small parties and candidates might be unwise in the long run, if its effect is to frustrate the rise of new viewpoints and potential "major" parties and candidates of the future. The Democratic and Republican parties were not always "major," and there may be potential future dominant parties waiting in the wings, more responsive to future national needs and interests than the vested political institutions of today.

Though the factual situations and circumstances will differ enough to prevent the setting forth here of pat rules for the guidance of the candidate, he should be alert to both the opportunities and the pitfalls awaiting him in the complex pattern of rules and regulations comprehended by both the "fairness" and "equal time" requirements.

In addition to the preceding considerations, the candidate should, of course, be aware that his utterances during the campaign, whether on the air, in print or in direct discourse, are governed by the laws concerning libel, slander and defamation. Two excellent sources of general information in these areas are Ashley's **Say It Safely** (revised ed., University of Washington Press, 1966) and a unit of the Legal Almanac series (No. 15, **Libel and Slander**, by Ella C. Thomas).

Concerning the Financing of Presidential Campaigns

As the costs of conducting election campaigns for the two principal national offices have risen steadily in the present century, the degree to which the major parties and candidates have become dependent on the contributions of large, powerful, wealthy special-interest groups has mounted proportionately. During the 1964 campaign, the Republicans were able, it is true, to tap the interest and pocketbooks of many small contributors, but this is partly attributable to particular ideological and emotional appeals exerted by the nominees of that year. Generally, the parties and candidates have been beholden in great degree to big business, big labor, and other large, strongly financed interests. In the belief that this trend is not wholesome for the strength, independence and well-being of the political system and government of the United States, President John F. Kennedy in 1961 appointed a bipartisan Commission on Campaign Costs which in 1962 issued a report that included five draft bills for submission to Congress. President Kennedy sent these bills to Congress in May 1962, accompanied by a statement in which he pointed out that the sources of financial support for Presidential candidates must be broadened so that millions of citizens have a part in supplying the increasing sums needed for modern campaigning. The employment of mass media, particularly television, has placed great financial burdens on the candidates and the parties. New sources of funds are needed, he felt. The approach of the five submitted bills, and other bills of later date offered in Congress, has essentially been that of using the tax machinery to provide incentives for citizens to contribute to campaign funds. The Kennedy commission suggested two alternative methods to be made available to the taxpayer, as follows:

(1) A tax credit against Federal income tax of 50 percent of contributions up to a maximum of $10 in credits a year, or

(2) A tax deduction for political contributions for the full amount of the contribution up to a maximum of $750 per tax return per year (the Commission had originally recommended $1,000).

Later proposals, advanced during the administration of President Lyndon B. Johnson, included one under which taxpayers, by checking a box on the income tax return form, could indicate a willingness that $1.00 of the income tax due be diverted to the credit of a fund from which the Treasury would make payments to the two principal political parties in equal amounts. The draft bills of this character included provisions under which minor parties could share in the payment only by showing that they had polled a relatively large minority percentage of the vote in previous campaigns. These bills proved highly controversial when debated in Congress, and as of 1968 none have been enacted into law.

Other features of the Kennedy commission's recommendations concerning political finance are of interest in showing the result of mature thinking on this problem in the 1960's:

(1) That voluntary bipartisan activity be encouraged, and efforts be made to remove the stigma attaching in popular thinking, all too often, to active participation in political movements;

(2) Tax incentives, as outlined above;

(3) That effective means be provided for full disclosure of campaign receipts and disbursements by candidates and parties and their instrumentalities;

(4) The removal of existing restrictions on the amounts individuals could contribute to campaigns;

(5) That partisan political contributions by corporations and labor unions be prohibited;

(6) That all laws retained in existence, and the new ones to be enacted, be enforced vigorously;

(7) That the parties develop effective means of making mass solicitations of small contributions from large numbers of citizens;

(8) That research programs be instituted to seek reductions in campaign costs;

(9) That the cost of making transitions between Administrations, after elections, be publicly borne and "institutionalized," so that these costs would not, as is now the case, fall to a large degree on the national party committees;

(10) That Section 315 of the Federal Communications Act be suspended during Presidential campaigns;

(11) That a White House Conference on campaign finance be held;

(12) That the states seriously consider adopting all or part of the national commission's recommendations; and

(13) That the operations of such reforms as are adopted be restudied after adequate trial periods.

The Electoral College System: Faults and Reforms

Space in this small work does not permit an extended treatment of the role played by the Electoral College system in choosing the President and Vice President. Briefly, each state is, under the Constitution, allotted a number of electoral votes equal to the sum of its Senators and Representatives in Congress. The popular vote of each state is actually cast for electors chosen by the political parties, which electors are morally obligated to vote for the Presidential and Vice Presidential nominees of those parties. The party which receives a plurality of the popular vote in a given state "carries" that state and receives all of its electoral votes. After the general election in November, the Electoral College (all the Presidential electors chosen by the voters) meets and casts its votes as directed by the popular vote result in each state. The result of the electoral voting, after being properly certified, is transmitted to the Congress in January before the appointed inauguration day (January 20) for a final official "counting." The effect has been that the vote by the Electoral College is a formality; all electors dutifully cast their votes for the chosen candidates of their states, except in very few instances where an elector has voted independently. The Constitution writers contemplated that the electors would act independently, and that the choice of a President by this means would take the selection of the Chief Magistrate out of the hands of the popular electorate and place it in the hands of wise, mature, persons who would vote for the most qualified candidate. In practice, with the rise of the party system, the broadening of the suffrage and the improvement of voter quality through increased education and more public information available concerning the candidates and platforms, the electoral system has become an expensive, cumbersome and dangerous anachronism. In many states, the names of electors do not even appear on the ballots or voting machines, but the electoral system must still be observed unless the Constitution is amended. The chief dangers inherent in the present system are:

(1) Since electors are legally empowered to vote as they please, there is no absolute assurance that their votes will actually be cast for the candidates chosen in their states by the popular vote; this danger is minimal, but is ever present and could affect the result in an extremely close election.

(2) The method is fairly effective under the present two-party system, but a major constitutional crisis could readily be precipitated if a strong third-party movement should develop and syphon away enough electoral votes to keep either major party from securing a majority in the Electoral College. In such event, the Constitution provides that the House of Representatives shall choose the President. Each state, in such an election, would have but one vote, regardless of its population or representation in the House. The candidate chosen through such a process could well be one selected by Representatives from states having small populations and, in no sense, the choice of the vast majority of voters in the populous areas of the country. Also, under the present system, it has happened in several cases that the President who was elected had an actual minority of the nationwide popular vote, but had electoral votes so distributed among the large states that he secured a majority in the College.

Many proposals have been advanced for amending the Constitution to either abolish the Electoral College altogether or to provide, by any of various means, that the electoral vote in each state be made reflective of the true size of the popular vote cast for each candidate. Perhaps the most carefully worked out and clearly expressed suggestions are those contained in the report of the American Bar Association's

31

Commission on Electoral College Reform, issued in January 1967, entitled **Electing the President**. Its recommendations would abolish the Electoral College altogether and provide for the election of the President and Vice President by direct, nationwide popular vote. Should no candidate receive 40 percent of the popular vote, a nationwide runoff election would be held between the two top candidates. The interested reader is referred to the report itself for further details on this constructive, carefully thought out set of suggestions.

Chapter 3

HOW PUBLIC OFFICE IS ACQUIRED—APPOINTMENT

Most of the foregoing has application to the process of seeking and securing election to office. But there is the remaining method of securing office—by appointment. What legal considerations apply to this process? If one examines the applicable statistics, it will be readily apparent that there are far more appointive public officials around than elective ones. This book cannot go into the subjective considerations that motivate the appointing power in choosing one person for office over another. Matters of qualification for the duties to be performed, of course, should be dominant in the thought processes of the appointing official. Also, "political" availability (harmony of thinking with the party and officials in power, political party record, and the like) will in almost every case be considered. Formal qualifications—age, place of residence, educational background, previous work history—will obviously play a part in the selection process. Other considerations concerning availability for appointive office come readily to mind. With these and like subjective considerations, this work cannot deal. Our discussion is confined to the situation of the person who has been selected for appointment. Excellent case histories have been written by scholars who have considered the forces bearing upon specific appointments of historical significance. One of these, A. W. Todd's **Justice on Trial**, concerns the appointment by President Wilson of Justice Louis D. Brandeis of the Supreme Court; another, D.J. Danelski's **A Supreme Court Justice Is Appointed**, gives the history of President Harding's appointment of Justice Pierce Butler to the same court. Both are interesting studies of the appointing process in action.

At the Federal level, appointment of persons to the higher public offices, and to the civil service generally, is provided for in the Constitution of the United States, Article II, section 2, which prescribes that the President "shall nominate, and by and with the advice and consent of the Senate, shall appoint ambassadors, other public ministers and consuls, judges of the Supreme Court, and all other officers of the United States, whose appointments are not herein otherwise provided for, and which shall be established by law; but the Congress may by law vest the appointment of such inferior officers, as they think proper, in the President alone, in the courts of law, or in the heads of departments." At the state level, the number of officials who are elected varies, from two or three in some states (Virginia is an example) to a large number of the principal statehouse offices and department heads in other states. In every case, however, the number who are appointed greatly exceeds the number elected.

Federal offices filled by Presidential appointment, with the "advice and consent" of the Senate, include all the Cabinet and sub-Cabinet offices, the heads and members of the Federal regulatory and administrative agencies (Interstate Commerce Commission and Federal Trade Commission, for example), heads of the independent Federal agencies not under Cabinet departments (for example, the Administrator of Veterans Affairs), directors or heads of Federal corporations such as the Tennessee Valley Authority and the Export-Import Bank, heads of agencies under the Legislative Branch where authorized by statute (such as the Public Printer and the Librarian of Congress), all of the judgeships of the Federal Courts (District Courts, Courts of Appeals, Court of Claims, Court of Customs and Patent Appeals, etc.), and principal offices below the sub-Cabinet level within the Cabinet departments. These latter include the Commissioner of Internal Revenue in the Treasury Department, the Director of the Federal Bureau of Investigation in the Justice Department, and others. Heads of a host of specialized agencies, both within and without the principal Cabinet departments, are appointed in like manner. Unless otherwise prescribed by statute or the Constitution (most Federal judges, for example, serve during "good behaviour" by Constitutional provision), the officers so appointed and confirmed serve during the pleasure of the President. This includes all the Cabinet and sub-Cabinet officers and heads of most agencies. In a number of cases, especially those of the regulatory and quasi-judicial agencies, the statutes creating the positions prescribe that the officers shall serve for stated terms, usually so arranged that only a portion of a plural membership rotates out of office at any given date. This insures a continuity of experienced leadership on the board, commission or like body. A later portion of this book discusses the termination of, and removal from, office of an appointee.

At the Federal level, when the President selects a person to fill a vacancy in an appointive office, or persons to fill openings in newly created bodies filled by appointment, he submits (if the positions are those requiring Senate confirmation) the name or names to the Senate, which refers them to the applicable committee concerned with the subject matter of the appointee's agency or position. For example, an appointee for the Interstate Commerce Commission would be referred to the Chairman of the Senate Committee on Commerce. This committee, in due course, schedules hearings on the appointment, to which it invites all interested persons, groups and organizations who may attend or submit statements or letters, pro and con, for the record. Testimony is taken, and any written statements or comments submitted are studied. The appointee himself is summoned and questioned during the hearings. The nature, length, thoroughness and content of the hearings varies widely, of course, depending on whether the appointment is routine in nature, controversial or non-controversial, whether the appointee is well known or obscure, what interests (commercial, professional, trade, industrial, etc.) are affected and how they view the appointment as helpful to or detrimental to their own causes. The hearings are printed at some future date, although in the case of "sensitive" or intelligence-oriented appointments (such as heads of the National Security Agency or Central Intelligence Agency), much of the testimony may be omitted from the printed record. The committee that held the hearings then makes its report to the Senate, which by a majority vote confirms or refuses to confirm the appointment. An officer appointed by the President to a position requiring Senate confirmation may serve in a recess appointment during a period that the Senate is not in session. During this time he may perform the duties of the office, take the oath and draw the prescribed salary; he may not continue in office beyond the next session of the Senate, however, unless duly confirmed.

Most state government positions at the higher levels, when filled by appointment, are treated in essentially the same way, so far as the confirmation procedure is concerned, although in many states no hearing records are printed.

A number of lower ranking Federal civil positions, of course, require Presidential appointment but do not require Senate confirmation. Some positions requiring Senate confirmation are considered routine to the extent that hearings are ordinarily not held. A principle of Senatorial courtesy is observed in these and other confirmation procedures. Under this principle, if a Senator from the state of the appointee objects to the nominee as "personally obnoxious" to him, confirmation is refused by the Senate. Usually, in such cases, the name is not even submitted for a formal vote.

The Power to Appoint to Office

The supreme power to govern, and therefore to appoint public officers, rests with the people under the American system. The people may, by the Constitution, prescribe the method of appointment, and delegate the power to the legislative, the executive or the judicial branch. The power to appoint has been generally considered an executive function or attribute, but this does not limit the exercise of the power to the executive officer or his deputies or department heads. Unless otherwise limited by the organic law, the legislative body may, in setting up offices for the public service, designate the person, body or agency to make the appointment or appointments. Whoever makes the appointment is required, by considerations of basic law and policy, to regard only the public good in selecting the person or persons for office. Courts will not enforce or recognize any contracts, bargains or agreements between an appointing officer or body and a prospective appointee, whereby such seeker of appointment is to be chosen or named in consideration of any payment of money, preferment or any thing of pecuniary value. Any consideration other than those of the appointee's fitness, fidelity, loyalty, competence and integrity would be void and of no effect on public policy grounds. The holder of the appointing power may not, for the same reason, bargain away or unlawfully delegate to another, the power and right to make the appointment. Counsel may be taken of others' views and advice may be sought, but the ultimate power of appointment rests with him to whom the law entrusts it. Where the law specifies particular qualifications which the appointee must possess, these of course may not be disregarded in selecting the person to hold the office. Even absent formal statements in the organic law, the appointing official must be guided by the nature of the duties to be performed in selecting an appointee. For example, the Constitution of the United States does not say that the Chief Justice must be a lawyer, nor that any judicial officer must be a member of the bar, yet it would be a foolhardy and obtuse President indeed who sent to the Senate for confirmation the names of any but the most able lawyers among those available for these offices.

Chapter 4
THE PUBLIC OFFICIAL IN OFFICE

Entry Into Office

If the candidate is chosen for elective office, he is duly certified as elected in the manner prescribed by state or Federal law, as the case may be. Assuming that all contests, recounts, canvasses, etc., have been satisfactorily resolved, the candidate goes through the process of "qualifying." This includes giving such assurances or undertakings as may be required that he meets the formal requirements for the office —age, citizenship, residence, etc.—and the posting of whatever bond is required for the office to be held. In virtually every office involving the direct or indirect handling of funds belonging to the agency or office involved, or of private funds, the keeping of records on which pecuniary consequences depend, or the performing of any duties involving public or private financial consequences, the posting of a bond is required. County sheriffs, tax collectors or commissioners, treasurers and county clerks, court clerks, referees in bankruptcy, license commissioners, water commissioners, state roads commissioners or highway board members, collectors of customs or excises and the like are only a few of the officials whose entry into and holding of office requires a bond as evidence of financial responsibility and as a protection to the government or agency against shortages and defalcations or loss of public funds. Careful inquiry must be made into the local, state or Federal regulations prescribing the bond; the amount, source of the bond and its exact nature, method of paying premiums (by the officeholder or from the public treasury), investigations to be made and data to be supplied by the bonded official; all these must be known and usually complied with before entry into office. Failure to post a satisfactory bond might well mean failure to take the office for which one has worked diligently through an election campaign. Likewise, continued tenure in an office once taken may be ended if a necessary bond should be revoked for any reason.

Status of the Public Official at Law

Once the candidate has qualified, posted whatever bond may be required and observed such other formalities as taking the oath of office, what is his status in contemplation of law? It must be remembered that under judicial determination, the public official holds an office whose duties are not prescribed by superior officeholders but are set out in the constitutional or statutory provisions creating the office and defining its purpose and functions. Should the position be one already in existence and occupied hitherto by one or more predecessors, there will be precedents and guidelines to follow; conditions will, however, arise where these afford small indication of what decision to make or what course to follow. One of the hallmarks of the true public office, then, is that a degree of independence, judgment and choice inheres in the position; a wise exercise of his powers of judgment and discretion is expected of the incumbent.

Fidelity and Loyalty

Very early in history, those sovereigns who created administrative and judicial and other offices set forth the requirement in stern terms that the incumbents owed an obligation of fidelity and loyalty to the sovereign power. Acts of disloyalty, inconsistent with this obligation, were punished severely. From the time of the New Testament, where it is pointed out that no man can serve two masters, it has been clear that the officeholder's primary allegiance is to the appointing or the electing power—the sovereign, by whatever name designated. The oath of office is the solemn, semi-dramatic means by which this obligation is impressed upon the new officer and made a matter of permanent record.

In the day-to-day performance of his functions, then, the official is to remember that while on duty and at all times, he shall so order his own affairs and those of his position that the two do not conflict. Sometimes, by statute or administrative edict, the officer is required to divest himself of such affiliations, holdings or assets, as would give rise to actual or apparent conflicts of his own interests with those of the public power he is sworn and obligated to serve. In practice, it is not always easy to determine when interests conflict; or, even more difficult, to determine when they might conflict. Much time has been devoted in recent years, in Congress, the state legislatures and in the executive and judicial branches of the Federal, state and local governments, to problems centering in the conflict-of-interest area. It can intrude at all levels of government and in many contexts; the newspapers rarely miss a day in which some example of actual or potential conflict of public and private interest of some official or body is not discussed or described. Examples are those in which a county board of supervisors, or zoning commissioners, awards a choice commercial or industrial or high-density apartment zoning classification to interests whose contacts with the awarding authority have been other than arms' length and aboveboard; government contracts awarded to other than the lowest or otherwise most suitable bidder; sums passed, or allegedly passed, under the counter from one seeking a favor to an official in a position to grant the favor; the mysterious paving of the driveway of a powerful local political or public figure by employees of the street or roads department, using publicly owned equipment; the mysterious and overly-rapid passage through a state legislature of an act greatly increasing the size and weight of trucks permitted to use the highways of the state—the examples are legion. They touch even the judiciary, of all branches the one most expected to operate with incorruptible integrity. Fortunately, in the latter category, the authenticated instances of actual judicial corruption are relatively few, and very few examples of such misconduct have stained the integrity of the higher state and Federal courts.

It is easy to set forth the pat statement that the public official must have no conflicting interests, that he must hold himself above suspicion, but it is hard in many actual cases to draw a clear line. Appointees to Cabinet positions have been required, before securing Senate confirmation and as a condition precedent thereto, to sell all their stocks in large corporations whose interests might conceivably conflict with those of the government department to be headed by the appointee. To what extent should a prospective official at this level be expected to make such sales, in the context, let us say, of a declining market? What of the problem of family holdings, trust funds, non-profit family foundations and the like? What tests will be applied to assure that the appointee be not unduly penalized and the public interest not prejudiced? What effect on the public service would there be if very strict requirements were imposed concerning privately held assets, and such requirements resulted in increasing difficulty in securing highly qualified persons to accept appointment to major offices? In many cases, the possible choices are limited; for certain agencies, the number of persons technically and educationally fitted for the appointment is not great, and all may well be the products of experience and training gained in private enterprise. Many have acquired, over the years, high corporate offices, interests in pension funds, deferred compensation, stock options and the like, that would mean severe personal and family sacrifice should they be compelled to divest themselves of all holdings and ties as a condition of confirmation to appointive office.

The foregoing are just a few of the difficult problems encountered in defining "conflict of interest" in the context of elective and appointive public office. With reference to elective office, it is clear that an elected candidate who is excessively obligated to special interests that financed his campaign is, however much he may seek to act impartially, stained with suspicion that he may have a loyalty to his political supporters that transcends the loyalty he owes to his governmental sovereign. This consideration, of course, is one that motivated President Kennedy in naming the Commission on Campaign Costs, and a consideration that motivated the Commission in urging on state and local governments that they consider major reforms in the financing of election campaigns in their areas. The more widely diffused among the electorate the financing of campaigns becomes, the less, obviously, is the likelihood of a person being elected who owes his success to special interests.

Misconduct in Office

Obviously, nonfeasance or malfeasance in office (the nonperformance or wrongful performance of duty) constitutes grounds for punishment, including removal from office and/or the penalties prescribed for criminal acts. Likewise, bribery, embezzlement, larceny, fraud and other acts that would be crimes in a private relationship are no less criminal when committed by a public official. We need not dwell on these obvious instances of misconduct.

Other acts, when performed by incumbents of offices of trust and responsibility, have been held to be unlawful, even when statutes did not specifically define them as crimes. For example, many years ago a Pennsylvania official, whose office issued land warrants and had custody of public land surveys and maps and records concerning land allotments, found a tract of land recorded whose survey and boundaries were not clearly set forth. The land had been claimed for many years, and taxes paid on it, by a lumber manufacturer who held it in good faith under a state warrant. The officeholder made a formal application to himself in his official capacity for a. land warrant in his own name; caused a survey to be made, accepted the return of survey and declared it valid, and finally caused a land patent to issue from himself, the official, to himself, the applicant. In a resulting legal action the high court of the state declared the self-dealing of the official to be unlawful. Said the court,

"It is true . . . that there is no enactment to be found in the statute book of this state which in

42

words forbids (the action described). But it does not follow that every thing may be done by a public officer that is not forbidden in advance by some act of assembly. Remedies are provided for evils when they are discovered, and rules of law are applied when a necessity arises for their application. What is alleged in this case, and was held by the learned judge of the court below, is that dealings between a public officer and himself as a private citizen that bring him into collision with other citizens . . . are against public policy. . . . Anything that tends clearly to injure the public health, the public morals, the public confidence in the purity of the administration of the law, or to undermine that sense of security for individual rights, whether of personal liberty or of private property, which any citizen ought to feel, is against public policy." **Goodyear v. Brown**, 155 Pa. St. 514, 26 Atl. 665 (1893).

Other courts have held, in early cases, that such actions as trafficking in and sale of public offices, borrowing in advance on the salaries of public offices, permitting strangers to perform the duties of offices after having "purchased" them from the lawful incumbent at a discount, levying on or attaching unpaid salary money in the hands of a fiscal officer before its payment to an official who is an alleged debtor—these and many more acts that would bring the public service into disrepute, cheapen or degrade the office and make it an article of commerce are invalid as against public policy.

Today, by statute and court ruling, the garnisheeing or attaching of Federal employees' salaries at all levels is unlawful. As a corollary, it should be pointed out that the Government does not look with favor on any tendency on the part of its employees at any level to abuse this immunity from attachment as a means of evading payment of just debts. Various administrative and disciplinary means are used to make a debtor in the public service realize, and act upon, the need to treat his creditors justly.

Does the Public Official Have a Property Right in His Office?

No. The office exists for the public convenience, interest and necessity, not for the benefit of the individual holding it. Very early in the history of American public office, the courts held that no vested right arose in favor of the incumbent, to the office he occupied. The sovereign power—state, local or Federal government—could by any lawful means abolish or change the office, relocate it geographically, alter its duties or functions, or deal with it in any manner consistent with law and with the public interest, and without relation to the incumbent. To hold otherwise, the courts pointed out, would mean that long after certain functions might cease to be necessary for the public service, after science and technology had advanced to higher levels, employees whose utility to the body politic had ended, would have to be kept on the payroll "and the government would have to become one great pension establishment on which to quarter a host of sinecures." It was recognized that constitutional or statutory provisions might provide for certain terms of office that could not be shortened except as provided by law, and even for effective lifetime tenure in some cases (for example, most Federal judgeships, which are held "during good behavior"), but absent such provisions, an inherent attribute of sovereignty is the power to dispense with agents and officials and employees when the public interest would so indicate. In sum, the incumbent of a public office has no contractual right or property right in the office which would be violated if the employing government should (in the absence of the provisions above) reduce the term of office, lower the rate of compensation, or abolish it altogether. English law formerly provided that certain offices did constitute "livings" or "incorporeal hereditaments" to which certain vested rights attached in favor of incumbents, and even their heirs and assigns, but in the United States after the Colonial period no such titles to office survived.

Since the establishment of the merit system in the early 1880's at the Federal level, and related or similar civil ser-

44

vice career systems at the state and local levels, of course, statutory protections of various kinds have been erected to eliminate considerations of political patronage and to prevent the taking of arbitrary, unjust or discriminatory actions against employees. These systems were established because it was recognized that the efficient day-to-day operation of the public machinery required a secure, selected, trained body of career workers who would not be put in fear of ouster for political reasons or grounds other than those of fitness and objective qualifications. None of these statutes, however, impair the inherent power of the sovereign to abolish positions or offices, reduce the forces hired, transfer or remove agencies or establishments, and the like. They merely provide safeguards to insure that such actions, when taken, will not discriminate unjustly against any person in the public service. In contemplation of law, no career civil service employee, or official under the merit system, enjoys a vested or property right in the position he holds.

One qualification is necessary in connection with the statement that a public office is not the property of the person who lawfully holds it at any given time. The lawful incumbent's right to discharge the duties and receive the emoluments of an office during his proper tenure is recognized as a right or privilege protected by law, and an office may be considered as property in disputes arising between two or more persons claiming the right to hold the same office. A public officer, lawfully engaged in the discharge of the duties of the office, is entitled to the protection of the law in any controversy arising with an interloper, usurper or other person not entitled to hold or occupy the office.

A public office is not property except in the limited sense described above; neither is it a contract or the product of a bargaining or negotiating transaction with the sovereign power. The courts have held, almost without exception, that no contract relation arises in favor of one who has been appointed or elected to a public office. Public contracts do, in fact, exist. The government may lawfully contract with individuals or corporations, firms etc., to supply it with goods and merchandise for public use or benefit, or for buildings, bridges, highways and public works generally. Those who receive public contracts to supply these goods and services are not public officers. Likewise, persons who contract with the public authority to perform specified personal services for which they are particularly fitted, such as painting murals in a public building or conducting a technical survey or study for a specified purpose, are performing a public service but are not public officers. The contract relationship, like the property right, is inconsistent with the concept of a public office as it has developed in this country.

Regarding Qualifications for Office

There are, broadly speaking, two chief types of public offices: constitutional and statutory. Constitutional offices are those set up and defined in the United States Constitution or in the state constitutions. As to these, the legislative bodies may make no fundamental changes without authority from the people in the form of constitutional amendments. The qualifications to hold such offices, their titles, tenure, compensation and other material attributes, when set forth in the constitution, are to be observed. Their existence and continuation are protected by the organic law until that law is validly changed. As to statutory offices, these are set up and may be altered, abolished, transferred, consolidated and otherwise changed by the legislative body in any manner sanctioned by law. This may be done without regard to the status or position of the incumbents, if any; that is, the legislative body is not bound to consider the individual incumbent in making major changes in the offices or in abolishing them altogether. The incumbent is not protected by any contractual relationship with the public authority that would militate against such alteration of his official status as the legislature may see fit to make, so long as such body acts within the constitution. The legislature may prescribe the qualifications for entering upon or holding such an office, the duties to be performed, the compensation to be received, the place of performing the duties, their territorial range and the tenure or term of such office. The legis-

lature may not alter the essential attributes of a constitutional office, but may do so with a statutory office.

When the courts have been called upon to consider cases
involving qualifications to hold public office, they tend to
construe broadly those clauses in the statute or constitution
that prescribe qualification, and to construe narrowly any
clauses that prescribe disqualifications (such as, for example,
prior conviction for felony or misdemeanor involving moral
turpitude). The tendency is, wherever lawfully possible, to
rule favorably upon the qualifications of the person laying
valid claim to the office, rather than to seek means and
methods of disqualifying him.

Qualifications imposed by the legislature on eligibility to
hold public office must bear some reasonable relationship to
the duties and functions of the office. The legislature may
not validly make arbitrary restrictions, such as those for age,
sex, occupation, education, place of residence and the like,
when such restrictions bear no clear relationship to the
actual office and the qualities needed for its proper discharge. No classes of the population may be arbitrarily barred from seeking or holding office, nor may the qualifications be so narrowly drawn as to constitute "tailoring" the
place for a particular applicant. Some qualifications once
widely regarded as valid in connection with state or local
office are now frowned upon as unduly restrictive, or as no
longer needed in an age of widespread education and a
highly mobile populace. For example, requirements that an
officeholder must hold property or pay taxes within a community, once very common, are now disappearing rapidly,
by court order, legislation, or constitutional amendment.
Religious tests, also once very widespread in the older parts
of the United States, are now almost nonexistent. Until
very recent years in Maryland, jurors, notaries public, and
other appointees, were required to affirm a belief in God
as a condition of serving. A court decision in a mandamus
case, declaring such test of belief unconstitutional, had the
effect of requiring a new trial for every person convicted
criminally by a jury, or upon the indictment of a grand jury,
whose members had been under the requirement of this test,
if such person petitioned for a new trial.

47

As to qualifications based on sex, contrary to widespread belief, the ratification of the Nineteenth Amendment to the United States Constitution did not automatically make women eligible for election to public office throughout the country. By eliminating denial or abridgment of the voting right on account of sex, it opened offices to women where the qualification prescribed by law limited eligibility to qualified voters or electors. However, where constitutional or statutory language at the state or local level expressly restricted office, or certain offices, to males, women remained disqualified. In recent decades, however, many of these provisions have been repealed or nullified, and it may be observed that generally in this country women are free to seek and hold elective or appointive office on the same terms as men.

An obvious disqualification, rooted in the old English common law and affirmed or strengthened in the constitutions and laws of many states, is the one prohibiting the holding of two "incompatible" offices by the same person at the same time. It is clear that the governor of a state may not at the same time serve as a judge on the state's supreme court or as its attorney general. Less clear are certain restrictions imposed by law against holding two or more offices, not limited to incompatible ones, at the same time. Some states forbid the holding of a state and a Federal office simultaneously; others, the holding of two or more positions of "trust" or "profit" or "honor" or "of emolument" at the same time. Generally, courts, recognizing that the holding of office is a valuable privilege, tend to construe such clauses narrowly so as to hold to a minimum the disqualification of persons, unless some clear consideration of public policy or public benefit makes it plain that the holding of plural offices in a given situation is unwise or undesirable.

In some cases, of course, the constitution makes clear the prohibition against certain classes of officers holding specified kinds of other offices. The United States Constitution, Article 1, section 6, clause 2, forbids any Senator or Representative holding any civil office under the United States during the time of his elected term of office, if the office was created or the emoluments thereof increased, during such term. Also, no person holding office under the United States may, under the same clause, be a member of either House during his continuance in the office. Similar, and sometimes more restrictive, provisions govern the office-holding of state legislators. Often they not only prohibit the holding of other state offices, but Federal, municipal and county offices during the legislator's elected term. All these restrictions are grounded upon the public policy consideration that a legislator should not be placed, or place himself, in a position where he could conceivably benefit from the results of legislation he had a part in passing. The power of the legislator to vote for an increase in his own legislative compensation lies inherently in the sovereignty of the legislative body, and is held in check by the force of public opinion. The opportunity to benefit from legislation affecting an agency in which he may hold another office is a different matter. It is an unnecessary and undesirable risk to which the body politic should not be subjected. Conflict of interest and of allegiance is obvious in such a situation.

The general rule is that a person who accepts, qualifies for and enters upon a second office that is incompatible with the one he already holds (or a second office from which he is otherwise barred by law) in effect vacates his first office and holds the second one. Normally under the common law, no court proceeding is necessary to formalize the vacating process. An election may be held, or a new appointee named, to fill the vacated office. The person, in accepting the second office, is said to have elected to hold, or chosen, the second office in preference to the one he held formerly; this despite what may be his expressed intention to hold both offices simultaneously. Where ineligibility to hold or accept the second office is clear, however, the rule is the opposite: the person remains an incumbent of his original position. A modification of the basic rule applies when one of the incompatible offices held or accepted is under a state or local government and one office is Federal. By reason of the sovereign position of the Federal vis-a-vis the state authority, the Federal office may not be declared vacant by a state authority. Normally the incumbent will become or remain a Federal officeholder and the state office will be vacant, regardless of the dates of entry into either.

Forbidden Acts, Generally

Much of the law governing conduct in public office is, of course, an expression of ethical and moral considerations that are widely accepted and approved in connection with the private conduct of business. However often they may be breached or evaded, they represent a received standard or norm of behavior, held up as an ideal to be striven toward. Various judicially pronounced and enforced principles have been written into the case law, and by the legislatures into the statute law, of the nation, the states and their subdivisions. Among these are:

1. Agreements for compensation to private individuals or public officials to procure contracts from the government to furnish its supplies, buildings, services or public works will not be enforced in the courts. The corrupting tendency of such agreements make them void on public policy grounds. They tend to introduce considerations into public dealings that differ from what should be the sole guide toward making these decisions; namely, who can best render the service or supply the goods in question at the lowest cost to the public treasury?

2. For the same reason, agreements to procure legislation for compensation are void. "These have been uniformly declared invalid, and the decisions have not turned upon the question, whether improper influences were contemplated or used, but upon the corrupting tendency of the agreements. Legislation should be prompted solely from considerations of the public good, and the best means of advancing it. Whatever tends to divert the legislators from their high duties, to mislead their judgments, or to substitute other motives for their conduct than the advancement of the public interests, must necessarily and directly tend to impair the integrity of our political institutions. Agreements for compensation con-

tingent upon success, suggest the use of sinister and corrupt means for the accomplishment of the end desired. The law meets the suggestion of evil, and strikes down the contract from its inception." **Providence Tool Co. v. Norris**, 2 Wall. 45 (1864).

3. Again, "the same principle has also been applied . . . to agreements for compensation to procure appointments to public offices. These offices are trusts, held solely for the public good, and should be conferred from considerations of the ability, integrity, fidelity and fitness for the position of the appointee. . . . Whatever introduces other elements to control this power, must necessarily lower the character of the appointments, to the great detriment of the public." **Id.**

Lobbying

The tendency of the law to frown upon the use of influence to secure services, offices or preferment of any kind from governmental sources extends, of course, to lobbying in the legislative bodies. However, practical controls of lobbying activities have proved difficult to implement or to enforce. The citizens are given, as a constitutional right, access to the public authority for the purpose of assembling and petitioning for the redress of grievances. Access may not be denied for the purpose of legitimately seeking legislation. It is exceedingly difficult to draw lines separating proper and improper means of influencing the legislative arm of the government. At the Federal level, an effort was made to control lobbying in the Congressional context, through an enactment passed in 1946 as part of the Legislative Reorganization Act. Cited as the "Federal Regulation of Lobbying Act" (60 Stat. 839-842, 2 U.S.C. §§ 261-270), it attempted to turn a spotlight of publicity on lobbying activities through a requirement that certain categories of persons and organizations seeking to influence legislation must register and render reports to Congress. "Lobbying" is considered as extending to "all substantial attempts to influence legislation for pay or for any consideration." It was hoped that by publicizing the sources and the extent of "substantial" financial support of lobbying activities, a degree of self-regulation and limitation of these efforts would be achieved without the need of imposing drastic penal sanctions (although a clause was included, prescribing imprisonment and/or fines for violations). By reason of loose and imprecise draftsmanship, it proved difficult to apply the act's provisions to actual lobbying activities and situations. The Supreme Court, in **United States v. Harriss**, 347 U.S. 612 (1954), in order to avoid declaring the applicable section unconstitutional as a violation of the free speech clause, interpreted the act as applying only to direct solicitation or "buttonholing" of Congressmen, and not as extending to a broad range of activities designed to secure or influence the passage or defeat of legislation in Congress. It is an accepted principle of law that any statute with criminal penalties must define the acts designated as criminal with precision, so that any person of ordinary intelligence can tell without doubt whether a given act does or does not fall within the forbidden area covered by ·the measure. Criminal prosecutions under the Federal Regulation of Lobbying Act ran afoul of this "vagueness" doctrine. Again, to save the act from unconstitutionality, a majority of the Supreme Court construed the law as proscribing only the soliciting, collecting or receiving of contributions of money for the purpose of influencing Congress directly, and not through any indirect means. Thus narrowly confined, the act was saved, but an immense range of communications with Congress financed with funds raised from special-interest groups, remains legitimate and beyond the act's limitations. Subsequent attempts to amend and strengthen the law have been unsuccessful.

State legislatures, even more than Congress, have been traditionally influenced by lobbying interests, and few states have been successful in limiting or effectively controlling this activity.

"Lobbying" in its invidious sense is to be distinguished from the rendering of professional services by attorneys and other representatives who seek to procure legislation to advance or secure some claim from a governmental agency or source. The Supreme Court has upheld the validity of contracts providing compensation for such services of a professional nature as "drafting the petition to set forth the claim, attending to the taking of testimony, collecting facts, preparing arguments, and submitting them orally or in writing, to a committee or other proper authority, and other services of like character. All these things are intended to reach only the reason of those sought to be influenced. They rest on the same principle of ethics as professional services rendered in a court of justice, and are no more exceptionable." **Trist v. Child**, 21 Wall. 441 (1874).

Lobbying Regulation—Various Proposals

Since in the broadest sense almost all publicizing of causes, doctrines and points of view to the end of creating a favorable climate of public opinion for or against the publicist's particular goal is lobbying, the effective regulation or curbing of such activity impinges directly on constitutional guarantees of free speech and free press. Various legislators and committees on the national scene have, since the unworkability of the 1946 Lobbying Regulation Act became apparent, sought for remedies that would insure effective disclosure of lobbying for specific legislation but would not curb or inhibit free expression of general views on public questions. Senator John F. Kennedy, in the late 1950's, sought to draft such a bill. The McClellan Committee (particularly with regard to political campaigns and contributions) also worked in this area. Because the 1946 act had sought to require registration and reporting from all whose "principal purpose" had been to influence legislation, many firms, corporations, unions, trade and professional associations and other groups, did not feel they must register since their "principal purpose" as they saw it, was far broader than the mere influencing of Congressional action. Weak means of enforcement, and inadequate publicity for such reports as were made, rendered the present act a virtual nullity so far as effective control is concerned. Proposals thus far submitted have included such means as broadly defining "influencing legislation" so as to include indirect campaigns (letter-writing drives and other grassroots activities) as well as the direct soliciting of Congressmen through buttonholing techniques. Dr. George Galloway of the Legislative Reference Service, Library of Congress, a long-time student of Congress, suggested that the law include a broad definition of "to influence legislation" but leave the enforcement of the act to the Justice Department, which he felt could be relied upon to screen specific occurrences so as to avoid prosecuting cases that might prove constitutionally vulnerable. It should be emphasized that no proposal has been advanced to prohibit lobbying altogether. All efforts are aimed at securing adequate reporting, information and regulation under which the sources of the pressures on Congress for or against specific legislation would be known to Congress and to the public. Such criminal penalties as are proposed are aimed, not at the act of lobbying or influencing legislation, but at violation of the registration and reporting requirements. Some of the bills aim both at securing registration and reports from the lobbyists themselves, and also from the true interests behind their lobbying activities, interests that are largely insulated from the light of publicity under the present act. Various proposals are included in the bills that would exempt the individual writer of letters to congressmen, and those whose expenditures and activities are so small as to remove them from the sinister connotations surrounding the massive campaigns, from the provisions of the suggested acts. Other proposals are that the act cover only campaigns aimed at specific legislation pending in Congress, not merely at the general effort to create a climate favorable to the publicist's point of view. By including these and other limitations, it is hoped that any new and corrective legislation would avoid the shoals of constitutional infirmity. The present act's unfair provision that radio and television stations must comply with the act's requirements, while newspapers are not covered, would also be eliminated.

Vacancies in Office: When and How Filled

Vacancies in public offices may occur at any time through

expiration of term of office, death, inability to perform the duties of the office, failure of an appointee to qualify, removal from office, resignation, impeachment, recall or by other means prescribed by law. The holding of or acceptance of an incompatible office, or a second office where two or more offices may not be concurrently held, as we have seen, may work a vacancy in one of the offices so held. A wholly new office, of course, is vacant. Whenever a vacancy validly exists, the proper authority may proceed to make a temporary or regular appointment to fill the vacancy. Usually, when the vacated office is elective in nature, the appointing authority may make a temporary selection of an incumbent to serve until an election can be held to fill the unexpired term. Most jurisdictions require the holding of a special election as soon as practicable to fill such offices, although in some cases the temporary appointee may serve out the unexpired term. In some cases, an office vacated through operation of law is simply not filled for the remainder of the term. For example, when the Vice President of the United States succeeds to the office of President upon the death, resignation or removal of the latter, the Constitution and laws make no provision for temporarily filling the office of Vice President. The office remains vacant until the next regular term begins. A new Vice President is chosen at the next quadrennial election, not in a special election. The duties of Vice President, those of presiding over the Senate, are discharged by the President Pro Tempore of the Senate, during the time the Vice Presidency remains vacant. The Presidential Succession Act prescribes a means of filling the office of President should a vacancy arise while there is no Vice President. The Speaker of the House, followed in order by other named officials, succeeds to the Presidency until the next regular term begins.

If an officer-elect or a chosen appointee dies before the commencement of his term, rulings have conflicted. Perhaps the prevailing rule is that the existence of a vacancy depends upon whether the deceased had qualified formally for the office before his death. If he has not, the usual practice is to permit the existing incumbent to hold over in the office as the temporary occupant until an election may be held or a new regular appointee named; this is followed in every case where constitution or statute provides that an incumbent shall serve until his successor shall have properly qualified. If the deceased dies after qualifying, the general rule is that a vacancy exists which may not be filled by the holdover method, since the incumbent's successor has properly qualified. In such cases, the appointing authority selects a temporary occupant of the office to serve until an election is held, or until a regular appointee is named.

Miscellaneous Provisions Governing Holding and Losing Office

TERM OF OFFICE—HOLDING OVER. The term of office is normally prescribed in the constitution, or it may be defined by statute. In the absence of constitutional restriction, the legislative body may prescribe the term. If neither the organic law nor statute set forth the term of an office, the general rule is that the appointing power may name an officer to serve at the former's pleasure. The policy of the law, as enunciated by the courts, favors occupancy of, rather than vacancy in, office; decisions generally favor procedures and practices that minimize the likelihood of and duration of vacancies. Thus, provisions concerning holding over of incumbents until their successors are properly qualified are looked upon with favor. When an incumbent holds over beyond his regular term, the law accords him all the powers and emoluments of the office until his successor is qualified and enters upon his duties.

WAYS BY WHICH OFFICE IS LOST:

1. Resignation: Unless otherwise provided for by law, a voluntary resignation is given effect upon its acceptance by the power that has the authority to name a successor. In the case of elective office, as we have seen, provision is made for temporarily filling the office until a proper election may be had to choose a successor, either for a new term or the remainder of an unexpired term. Generally a resignation

once accepted may not be withdrawn or rescinded by the resigning officer. If a resignation is offered or tendered, but not accepted, no vacancy exists, by general rule.

2. Abandonment: To work an abandonment of office, the position must be totally deserted by the incumbent. Moving from the jurisdiction or changing residence (when place of residence is a factor in eligibility for the office) so as to negate a condition of eligibility, works an abandonment. Refusal or failure to perform any of the duties of office serves as abandonment. Mere temporary absence from the jurisdiction will not normally result in a finding of abandonment. The intention of the incumbent, based on his observed acts, manifests the desire to abandon, or to hold, the office.

3. Impeachment: Most states follow the basic pattern of the United States Constitution in regard to impeachment. All but one of the states have a two-house legislature. Normally the lower house will impeach; that is, will prefer charges against an officer. It will do this by adopting articles of impeachment, alleging grounds that under the organic law will justify removal from office if proved. These usually include bribery, treason or "high crimes and misdemeanors" in office. The impeachment articles are filed with the upper house. The latter house sits as a court of impeachment and tries the case under prescribed rules of procedure. Since the legislative body is acting as a court, rules of evidence and other formal requirements must be observed. Since the action is a criminal trial, guilt must be proved beyond a reasonable doubt. A finding of guilty may normally not be appealed to the regular courts. The punishment almost always is limited to removal from office, sometimes with an added bar to holding any office of honor, trust or profit in the gift of the state. Since the officer under charges is suspended from the performance of his duties until the case is finally resolved, provision is made for temporarily filling the vacancy during the period of such suspension. A finding of not guilty will, of course, result in a restoration of the officer to duty. Both executive and judicial officers are subject to the impeachment procedure. Often, impeachment is the sole weapon for the removal of unfit judges, where the jurist

serves, as in the Federal courts, during "good behaviour." In most cases this actually means he serves for life or until he chooses to retire.

4. Removal: Usually, when an office is statutory rather than constitutional, the legislature is empowered to fix grounds for removal. It may also specify the removing authority, such as the governor; it may exercise this power itself in some cases. Legislative removal is sometimes called "address" and is provided for by constitutional authority in some states. A joint resolution, or other formal legislative action, will serve to remove an official by "address" or its equivalent. Sometimes, the right of removal is said to inhere in the right of appointment. In such cases, the appointing power is clothed with the power to remove for cause. Where no term is prescribed, removal is often at the pleasure of the appointing authority. Constitutional or statutory safeguards will often exist, however, to prevent arbitrary or capricious removals of officers. Sometimes the mere act of appointing a successor operates to vacate the office and displace the incumbent. The chief executive normally must have either statutory or constitutional authority to remove officers; he does not possess this power as an inherent attribute of his office. Courts and judges normally do not have a general removal power, though they may be empowered to name and to remove court officials and functionaries. Removal may be accomplished by "legislating out of office," under which the legislature may abolish an office, thereby abrogating the powers and duties of an officer. It may create a new office to perform the general functions of the abolished office, providing for a new method of choosing an occupant, and the like. Courts may invalidate mere "colorable" actions of this type, however, where the obvious purpose is to eliminate an individual or board of officers. Such enactments are valid where a clear purpose is shown to change the character or nature of the functions. In all cases, the legislature is limited and governed by constitutional restrictions. A constitutional officer may not be legislated out of office, nor may his salary or duties be changed in contravention of the fundamental law.

A legislative body is usually given power, under the constitution, to be the judge of the qualifications, fitness, and conduct of its own members, and may expel or exclude a member or a member-elect for cause which it deems sufficient. However, a recent Supreme Court decision has had the effect of limiting the power of a state legislature to exclude a member-elect when it is shown that the exclusion is based on infringement of United States Constitutional guarantees of free speech. In the case of **Bond v. Floyd**, 385 U.S. 116 (1966), the Supreme Court ruled that it could invade .the hitherto sacrosanct citadel of a legislature's discretion to determine the qualifications of its own members. Under the separation of powers and checks-and-balances system, courts had up until then held aloof from looking into the propriety of legislative decisions in this regard. However, in the **Bond** case, an allegation was made that a Negro elected to serve in the Georgia Legislature had been wrongfully excluded from his seat by reason of his outspoken exercise of freedom of speech. Bond had uttered sentiments in opposition to the United States involvement in the Vietnam conflict; these were thought by the legislature to show conduct inconsistent with the oath of office, which required the member to swear that he would support the Constitution and laws of the United States and of the state. The Supreme Court brushed this objection aside, apparently on a showing in the record that Bond considered himself able to support the Constitution despite his anti-war stand. It is significant that while the High Court acted to protect the claims of this member-elect of a state legislature, it continued to honor the separation of powers tradition in the case of Congress. When the House of Representatives excluded Adam Clayton Powell from membership in 1967, the Court refused to review the case on petition for a writ of certiorari. This action, while not a judgment on the merits of the case, evidently indicated that the tribunal would not depart, in the case of Congress, from the traditional position, even when constitutional reasons are alleged in a plea against exclusion. **Powell v. McCormack**, 266 F. Supp. 354, cert. denied 387 U.S. 933 (1967). In each case, the applicable constitutional provisions were similar, vesting each house with the power to judge the elections, returns and qualifications of its own members.

The law would thus seem to stand that, subject only to Federal Bill of Rights limitations in the case of state legislatures, any legislative body is the judge of the fitness and qualifications of those holding or claiming membership. A justification for the departure from tradition in the state case would be, that to subject a legislator to a stricter standard of speech restraint than the Constitution extends to private citizens, would be an unjust inhibition of freedom to debate and discuss issues in the house. Abstention in the Congressional case might be explained on the record which showed that, while constitutional grounds were urged by the excluded Congressman, the gravamen of the offense charged by the excluding body was a record of moral and financial dereliction, misuse of public funds, and the like. It remains to be seen whether a clear-cut Bill of Rights case, as in the state situation, would move the Court to enter the political arena vis-a-vis a House of Congress.

5. Forfeiture: There are few grounds for forfeiture of office in this country. Usually this occurs only when the law specifies that upon conviction of certain crimes, or other types of misconduct, an office may be forfeited. Forfeiture may or may not result from actual conviction, depending on the wording of the applicable provision.

Grounds for Removal or Loss of Office

Space does not permit detailed discussion of these grounds. They may include: misfeasance (the performance of a legal act in an improper or illegal manner); malfeasance (performance of acts themselves illegal); nonfeasance (failure to perform, or neglect of, duty); inefficiency, incapacity and immorality; corruption in office; extortion; misuse of or wrongful taking of money; habitual drunkenness or extreme intemperance; crimes generally, especially felonies or misdemeanors involving moral turpitude; and in some cases, acts connected with the procurement of the office which manifest illegality or impropriety reflecting on the officer's fitness to discharge his duties.

Proceedings for Removal

In order to prevent capricious or arbitrary removals, usually safeguards are set up in the law, even in cases not covered by civil service or merit statutes. Right to a notice in a prescribed form, and to some form of hearing, is usually given. Enough time is normally required between notice and hearing to afford some opportunity to prepare a defense. Counsel is generally permitted to represent the accused official. Proceedings may be quasi-judicial, with reasonable safeguards to insure fairness. All constitutional and statutory requirements are to be scrupulously observed. Judicial review, while by no means universally provided for, is often available to test the sufficiency, constitutionality and regularity of the proceedings. Some kinds of officers in some states may be removed only by judicial action. Usually, during the pendency of administrative or judicial proceedings looking toward an officer's removal, such person is suspended from the office he holds, and may not perform any of the duties. Such suspension may be with or without salary or emoluments, as provided by law.

Other Means of Losing Office

Obviously, death works a loss of office. Retirement, as provided by statute, will result in loss of office (but in case of judges and other officers serving during good behavior, retirement may not prevent the retiree's assisting in official capacities as his desires and abilities, and the needs of the service, may permit). The operation of recall proceedings, in some states, may result in loss of office. Under this system, a popular referendum is held upon the filing of a valid petition, usually one signed by a stated percentage of the electorate. A recall election must then be held as provided in constitution or statute, and the result of the election determines the officer's continuance in or loss of his office. This provision exists mainly in certain western states; there is no counterpart at the Federal level.

Disputes Concerning Proper Holder
of Office: Quo Warranto

In England, when the Crown had in its gift all public offices, one of the high prerogative writs was developed to enable proper authority to oust usurpers and pretenders from offices. This writ, called quo warranto, ranked with certiorari, mandamus, habeas corpus, prohibition, injunction and others as a prerogative of the Sovereign to be used for extraordinary purposes and contingencies. In this country, a proceeding called an information in the nature of quo warranto has superseded the old writ. As generally applied, it empowers the people of the state to proceed through the attorney general (or in some cases a prosecuting, county, city, circuit or district attorney) to file a legal action in the courts to test the right or title of one purporting to hold an office or a corporate franchise, or other benefit in the gift of the public. Generally, also, a private individual having a definite interest in the office in controversy (usually a rival claimant) may with the consent of the proper legal officer and by leave of court have an action filed by the state or the people on his behalf as "relator" (plaintiff) against the incumbent (called the "respondent"). Contrary to usual legal practice, in these cases the burden of proof, that is, of establishing title and right, is placed not on the plaintiff-relator, but on the defendant-respondent. Thus, the one occupying the office must by clear and affirmative evidence show that he has a prior or overriding right to hold and discharge the functions of the office. The action is in effect one to try the title to the office. It is usually held that citizens at large, and taxpayers, do not have such an interest in the office or its occupant as to entitle them to file such an action. In some states, where the proper attorney in office refuses, without good grounds, to file the action, citizens may be permitted to enter the case as plaintiffs, either in quo warranto or analogous proceedings. Some states, by statute, have eliminated the words "quo warranto", from the action, but the nature of the action survives throughout the nation. It is rarely used at the Federal level, since most appointments are made by Presidential action; few offices are held by election, and title and right to occupy the station is generally clear. In 1937, efforts by citizens to contest the right of Mr. Justice Black to occupy his Supreme Court seat on the ground that Mr. Justice Van Devanter's retirement (rather than resignation) from the Court had not created a vacancy, failed because the courts held that the would-be plaintiffs did not have such an interest in the office as would entitle them to proceed against the incumbent.

In successful actions of this nature, the remedy consists of the issuance of a writ of ouster by the court. This displaces the incumbent, but may not, in and of itself, establish the title or right of another to the office. A claimant to the office must show, not only that the former occupant was not entitled thereto, but that he himself has the full right and title to hold the office. This may in some cases require a separate action. While the quo warranto action has the form of a criminal proceeding, it is now rare that criminal penalties are assessed; generally this is only in the form of a fine and is assessed normally only when the attorney general or other proper officer has proceeded on his own motion in the name of the state, without the presence of a citizen-relator. Leave of court to file the action is not required where the proper attorney-official proceeds on his own motion in the name of the state or of the people.

Compelling Action by
Public Officer: Mandamus

If a public official, being required by the terms of his office to perform some particular duty incumbent upon him by law, fails or refuses to perform such duty, a legal remedy originating in early English practice lies to compel him to take the proper action. The writ of mandamus, like quo warranto, was originally a high prerogative writ vesting in the Crown. It may be defined, in its modern form, as a command or order issued by a proper court having jurisdiction, in the name of the state or sovereign, addressed to a public authority, officer, inferior court, board or other entity, directing the performance of some duty imposed by operation of law and lying within the official functions of the office or entity concerned. The writ lies to require a positive act, not to prevent or stop the performance of an act. The duty required under the writ must usually be ministerial in nature; that is, not an act which by its character or under law is discretionary or judicial. Examples of functions which may be directed by mandamus are: issuance of commissions to duly appointed or elected and qualified officeholders; holding an election at the proper time and place specified in the writ; paying interest on municipal or state bonds; paying out public monies upon presentation of proper warrants or vouchers; paying salaries to public officers or employees; signing deeds for the conveyance of land; duly authenticating bills passed by the legislative body and signed by the governor or passed over his veto; (in the case of a court) entering judgment in a case that has been properly tried and decided; and reinstating a wrongfully discharged civil service employee. Mandamus lies to enforce existing rights vesting in the person or body seeking the remedy, and will be used only when the performance of the desired act by the officer concerned will correct an abuse, right a wrong, and further rather than injure the public interest. A person having the power to act in a given situation with discretion may, by mandamus, be compelled to make a decision, but he may not be forced to decide the cause in a particular way or manner—if he has the power to decide, he still decides which way the judgment or choice will go, not the court issuing the writ. The writ merely forces him to make a decision rather than procrastinate. If the decision reached is erroneous, other remedies are available to correct it. Absent fraud, caprice or oppression, mandamus will not control discretion.

As with quo warranto, the requirement exists that only those persons who have a direct and immediate interest, transcending that of the public or taxpayers at large, may invoke the aid of the courts in mandamus proceedings. For example, citizens may not seek the writ to compel a city council to enforce a validly enacted but ignored ordinance (e.g., for the regular collection of trash) because they could not show that they are peculiarly injured by the nonperformance any more than residents of the city generally. However, a citizen whose home is particularly singled out and ignored by the trash collectors, while his neighbors enjoy regular collection, may (upon a showing that he has made a proper demand for service and refusal thereof) go to court to require proper trash collection as provided by law. Common or public nuisances, or abuses of public functions applicable to the community generally, may usually be corrected by the proper legal officer of the jurisdiction, in a proceeding instituted in the name of the people, the city or the state or county, as applicable. If the writ of mandamus is issued, and the offending official continues to refuse or fail to perform as directed without proper grounds, the court's contempt power is brought to bear; also damages may be assessed.

Chapter 5

LIABILITY OF PUBLIC OFFICERS

Basic Rule

No public officer, by reason of his status as such, is relieved from most of the rules of civil and criminal liability that apply to every citizen. In various contexts, we have seen that officers may be punished by removal, prosecution and in other ways for acts of wrongdoing. This chapter sets forth the basic rules covering specific types of criminal and civil penalties for wrongful acts of public officers.

Criminal Liability

If a public officer commits a crime, he is criminally liable; his crime is an offense against society and against the state. Our discussion is confined here to specific situations, other than obvious crimes (extortion, bribery, fraud, larceny, etc.) that have been implicitly or explicitly treated in previous contexts. Title 18 of the U.S. Code, the Federal Criminal Code, includes sections making it a crime for two or more persons to "conspire to injure, oppress, threaten or intimidate any citizen in the free exercise or enjoyment of any right or privilege secured to him by the Constitution or laws of the United States." Another section particularly covers those purporting to act as public officers: "Whoever, under color of any law, statute, ordinance, regulation or custom wilfully subjects, or causes to be subjected, any inhabitant of any State, Territory, or District to the deprivation of any rights, privileges or immunities secured or protected by the Constitution and laws of the United States . . . shall be fined not more than $1,000, or imprisoned not more than one year, or both." These sections are part of a series of acts passed in the Reconstruction era following the Civil War, and were designed to implement the three amendments

66

(the 13th, 14th, and 15th) placed in the Constitution to insure basic rights of freedom and citizenship for Negroes. The acts proscribed are personal and individual acts, or those of groups of conspirators, not the acts of states or other political units. Only officers de facto or de jure can act "under color of law." Court decisions have applied the penalties of these sections to such wrongdoers as perpetrators of nonviolent crimes (false or wrongful counting of ballots cast by Negro voters) and to violent crimes against arrested Negro prisoners. The former case was **United States v. Classic**, 313 U.S. 299 (1941); the latter was **Screws v. United States**, 325 U.S. 91 (1945). One case was decided on the basis of the right to vote secured by Article I, section 2 of the Constitution; the other under the Fourteenth Amendment. The latter amendment is directed against state action, but the Court majority found that a state officer (in this case, a sheriff) acting under color of law, was acting for the state; in mistreating a prisoner whose rights were protected by the amendment, he was committing an act of the state that deprived the victim of the rights to due process, equal protection, and privileges and immunities secured to him by the amendment. Dissenting Justices in the **Screws** case emphasized that such phrases as "due process" and the like are too vague to be made the basis, without more, of criminal charges under the applicable sections of the Criminal Code. Federal crimes are properly those defined in specific acts by the Congress, not indefinite concepts that shift with changing court interpretations over the years. In both the cases above, state officers violated state laws. In addition they were held to have violated the applicable portions of the Federal criminal laws. Does an officer of a state still act for his state when he wilfully disobeys the criminal laws of that state? The state may, of course, ratify and thereby become responsible, for the criminal act if it knowingly fails or refuses to punish the offender for his crime. If the state does not adopt, sanction, or ratify the act of the officer, then it would appear the better reasoning to say the officer acts in this instance as an individual only. The Fourteenth Amendment cannot reach individual action unless it may somehow be held to be state action. Because of the murky state of the law in this area, moves are under way at this writing (1968) to strengthen the Federal Civil Rights acts to define more explicitly what actions, and by whom, are criminal in the civil rights context. Most of this latter thrust is designed to secure the safety and protection of those who seek to exercise their rights guaranteed them under the Constitution and its amendments and implementing statutes (voting, holding office, enjoying equal accommodations, and the like).

Civil and Custodial Liability

Other sanctions prohibit wrongfully dealing with, or unlawfully removing, official records and other public property in the officer's care; of course, where (as is usually the case) a bond has been posted, the officer and the insuror or sureties on the bond are liable for unlawful conversion or other misdealings with public funds or property.

Generally, good faith or good motives do not relieve the officer if he is guilty of misfeasance or nonfeasance; also, if charged with injuring another through a negligent act, motives of good faith are immaterial.

An important distinction is made by the law at this point: an officer is held responsible for injury to others when he is exercising a ministerial function, but not when performing a discretionary act. A ministerial function is one required by law to be done under definite rules covering time, method or manner, and occasion of its performance, with such certainty that nothing remains for judgment or discretion. Action that results from performing a certain and specific duty arising from fixed and designated facts, is ministerial action. The negligent driving of an official car or truck; negligently discharging a firearm (by a peace officer) resulting in injury to a bystander; and unnecessary force in making an arrest, all have been held to make the officer liable. In some cases, a valid defense arises when the act is in obedience to the direct orders of a superior officer.

The higher public officers are concerned less with liability for ministerial acts than they are with the law covering discretionary acts. Some things cannot be done by unvarying written rules; they must be adapted to times and situations that are continually changing. If an officer is acting within the scope of his duties, he is generally not civilly liable for his acts of a discretionary nature, however erroneously or negligently he may perform them. (Needless to say, an incompetent officer does not have complete immunity. There are ways of getting him out of office). Judges, for example, are held through long precedent not civilly answerable for their judicial actions, even when they exceed their jurisdiction, or when they are said to have been done maliciously or corruptly. If a judge has no jurisdiction at all over the person or the subject matter of the case, he may have the status (with regard to those parties) of a mere usurper or interloper, and therefore be liable, if he presumes to rule in the matter. Impeachment, or defeat at the polls if the office is an elective one, are often the only remedies, if the judge acts wrongfully within his jurisdiction and in the course of his duties.

This doctrine has been extended to cover non-judicial superior public officers, who in performing discretionary acts are said to be acting judicially and are entitled to the personal immunity accorded judges. **Wilson v. Mayor**, 1 Denio (N.Y.) 595 (1845). Even the absence of probable cause and the presence of malice or other bad motives are not sufficient to impose liability on such an officer who acts within the general scope of his authority. **Cooper v. O'Connor**, 99 F. 2d 135 (App. D.C., 1938).

Acts that are clearly beyond the scope and functions of an officer's jurisdiction or proper cognizance are called ultra vires acts. A judge who issues a false warrant, knowing it to be false; a prosecuting attorney who arrests an innocent person without a warrant upon the unverified report of a private detective; a police officer using the "third degree" after an arrest—all are performing ultra vires acts, and acts for which they would be liable in false arrest, false imprisonment, or other appropriate actions.

What is judicial, and what is ministerial, in a given set of facts, may not be easy to determine. Often statutes and courts place a shield of immunity over officers at all levels who act in good faith and without malice in the performance of functions within the ordinary scope of official duty. Officers are liable for gross misuse of power, even when it is discretionary. The law is in conflict in cases where a subordinate officer acted in obedience to superior orders, and it later developed that the superior had no authority to issue the order. The better rule here would be to immunize a subordinate who had no way of judging the illegality of the order (he could be hardly expected to challenge a boss's ruling, having apparent validity).

A superior public officer is generally not responsible personally for the negligent, wrongful or faulty performance of duty by his deputies or subordinates. Nor is he responsible for their misfeasances or positive wrongs. The general legal rule, that the superior or principal is answerable for the acts and omissions of his agents or subordinates, has no application in the public officer context, except in very limited areas.

De Facto Officers

It sometimes happens that a person enters upon an office and performs some or all of the duties appertaining thereto, and yet because of some fault in the appointing or electing process, some overlooked or imperfectly performed formality, or a defect or invalidity in the law or statute setting up the office, it develops that the purported officer does not actually hold the office, the office itself does not legally exist or its existence ceases during the holder's presumed tenure or term. In such cases, citizens dealing in good faith with the person presumably in office need protection against adverse legal consequences flowing from the incumbent's decisions or acts. For this reason, such persons, who have held office under some color or appearance of right, are said to be officers de facto. As to the public generally, and citizens relying on the actuality of the office and the holder's apparent authority to serve therein, his acts and rulings are given a degree of validity. The appearance of authority may, in other words, be made actual authority, for some purposes. A person who believed, on presumably valid grounds, that he was sheriff of a county, and who was accepted as sheriff by the courts and by the public, may be a de facto sheriff, even though for some legal reason he either never held the office, or the office itself may not have had a legal existence during his supposed incumbency. Thus, the public and the courts are protected from the consequences of invalidity of the supposed sheriff's acts. Property on which he levied under legal authority from the courts, persons he arrested and jailed, and processes or summonses he served may be held to have been validly dealt with by the de facto officer. To hold otherwise would be to consign to chaos some, perhaps many, official acts, sales, arrests, services and other dealings. Some element of good faith, reliance, public acquiescence and actual performance of duty under apparent color of right are usually said to be required to make a person an officer de facto. A mere naked usurper or pretender to office, who acts in some capacity in the knowledge that he has no right so to act, does not acquire de facto status, and his acts are almost always said to be nullities. Only in cases of extreme public hardship would any legal consequence be allowed to attach to his acts. The opposite of de facto is de jure. An officer de jure has a legal right to his office.

With regard to de facto officers, the prevailing rule is that the protection afforded and the validity conferred on his acts operate only with reference to the public and to persons having official dealings with him as a supposed officer. The protection does not extend to the de facto officer as a person. Thus, while a person who buys a piece of property under a sheriff's sale conducted by the de facto officer is in law treated as a bona fide purchaser and protected in his title to the land, the de facto sheriff is not protected as an individual from a lawsuit and resulting judgment recovered by the former owner of the property. Recovery may be had against him as one who unlawfully converted the owner's property. There is a public policy reason why his presumably official acts should be given validity as regards the public and innocent third parties, but there is no policy ground for insulating the individual from the consequences of his own wrongful dealings. Authority exists to the contrary. Some courts, called upon to decide the consequences of a de facto officer's acts on him personally, have ruled in favor of the officer where his acts were done in good faith and in the belief that he was in fact an officer. This is on the ground that good, honest, highly qualified persons would not seek public office if they feared that by reason of some obscure technicality or flaw in the title to office they may not only find themselves out of office but mulcted in damages by persons with whom they had had official dealings during their period in purported office. The particular facts of a given situation, and the equities as between the contending parties, as well as the public good should guide the courts in decisions of this kind.

Chapter 6

DEVELOPMENTS IN CIVIL
AND CRIMINAL LIABILITY

Space permits only a brief treatment here of key recent developments:

1. In the area of the public official's redress against those who would defame his name and reputation in public; and

2. In the liability of a legislator for utterances he makes on and off the legislative floor.

No discussion of the basic law of libel and slander will be given. Traditionally, in most states, the public official has stood in essentially the same relationship to those who defame or slander him as other citizens. If his reputation and standing in his office were falsely impugned and traduced by printed or spoken defamatory utterances, he could go to court and recover damages for the tort (civil wrong) from the originator of the offense. A degree of privilege attached to utterances in derogation of an official; if the statements could be proved as true, the defense prevailed and no damages were recovered. If the statements proved to be false, usually the offended official recovered actual, and in some cases punitive, damages. The defendant's knowledge that the utterances were false need not be shown; actual falsehood in the public attack warranted recovery. Thus stood the prevailing law until 1964.

The Defamed Police Commissioner
and the Supreme Court

In the early 1960's, at the height of civil rights agitation in Montgomery, Alabama, an advertisement was published in the **New York Times**, sponsored by citizens' groups and a few Alabama ministers. It called attention to alleged acts of oppression committed against Rev. Martin Luther King and other civil rights workers. Allusion to official misconduct by law enforcement agencies in Montgomery, although couched in general terms, caused the commissioner of police in that city to bring suit against the newspaper and the Alabama Negroes for libel. He asserted that he had been injured in his name and reputation by the claims in the advertisement that police action or inaction had brought about alleged mistreatment of Negroes. In the resulting trial, it was shown, and admitted by the defense, that much of the supposedly factual material in the ad was false. Moreover, the **Times** admitted that material in its own files at the time the ad was published would have shown its falsity. The trial court entered judgment on a jury verdict for $500,000 damages and the Alabama Supreme Court affirmed. Sufficient malice was adjudged to warrant a large verdict, greatly in excess of what could have been recovered under a criminal libel action. Upon review by the United States Supreme Court, the award was reversed. Although this was a private lawsuit between a citizen and those he felt had defamed him, the High Court stated that it had jurisdiction to consider the appeal and apply the Free Speech clause via the Fourteenth Amendment, on the ground that the State of Alabama was involved through the application of its laws and the use of its courts in awarding the damages. The Alabama law of libel, the Court said, in this case operated to inhibit freedom of public expression through holding over those who would speak out on controversial public subjects, the fear that they would be penalized through the award of excessive damages, should it be shown that statements in derogation of an official were factually erroneous. The Court majority, speaking through Mr. Justice Brennan, held that a defendant in such a case should not be put to the requirement of showing that his statements were in fact true. The public interest in vigorous, robust and sharp discussion of public officials and their actions overrode the consideration of possible harm to them as persons and officers through the public utterance of defamatory falsehoods by their traducers. Only on a showing of actual malice could damages be recovered by an injured official. "Actual malice" was defined as follows:

"The constitutional guarantees require, we think, a federal rule that prohibits a public official from recovering damages for a defamatory falsehood relating to his official conduct unless he proves that the statement was made with 'actual malice'— that is, with knowledge that it was false or with reckless disregard of whether it was false or not."

The Supreme Court majority, in effect, applied what had hitherto been a minority rule among the state courts, that recovery could be had only upon such a showing of actual malice. **New York Times Co. v. Sullivan**, 376 U.S. 254, 282 (1964).

By defining malice in this sense, so as to include only a test of knowledge and/or recklessness, the Court eliminated the traditional definition of malice, which included elements of animus, dislike, hatred, or intent to harm and injure. Even so, three of the Justices would have gone further and eliminated even the "actual malice" requirement, thus rendering the offended official powerless to vindicate his name through any civil action against his detractors. Some observers have suggested that such an official should be afforded some guaranteed "right of reply," through which he could use similar media to refute the attacks against him as his defamers had used. (A sort of equal time or equal press space provision, perhaps?) It is axiomatic, however, as Hitler and many others have demonstrated through history, that a reply to falsehood never succeeds in overtaking and negating the lie itself. Actually, an offended public official usually has ready access to the press and the airwaves to answer his critics. One may wonder if this is sufficient to afford redress in these cases.

Since the **New York Times** case, the Court has extended the basic rule to cover libelous utterances against public functionaries at a much lower level than the traditional "public official," saying that anyone who performs public duties, and becomes subject to intense citizen interest, may find himself fair game for critics and their sometimes untrue and derogatory comments. **Rosenblatt v. Baer**, 383 U.S. 75 (1966), concerned the operator of a publicly owned ski resort, employed by a park authority. Still other cases have extended the privilege to detractors of persons who are not officials or even public employees: private citizens who have injected themselves into public controversies (e.g., Linus Pauling; Maj. Gen. Edwin Walker, U.S.A. Ret.), and private citizens who by reason of their callings or events occurring in their lives, have become "public figures" of a sort. This indicates the wide range of the Court's regard for freedom of vigorous public discussion and criticism of newsworthy personages.

The Case of the Bought Congressman

It has long been held that an absolute privilege attaches to public officials who speak on matters of public concern, in the exercise of and within the scope of their duties, so far as civil actions in the defamation area are concerned. If they speak outside the scope of their duties, they become liable for defamatory utterances the same as other persons. Also, if the comments are wholly unwarranted, the protection is lost. Often the protection of absolute privilege is granted only to governors and the highest state executive officials. Privilege also extends to legislative and judicial proceedings, and to acts of state, including communications made in the discharge of public duties and functions under law. This protects public transactions, and permits (among other things) freedom to keep candid and accurate personnel records. All the foregoing applies to civil liability for libel, slander, and defamation generally.

With regard to Congress members and to state legislators, a different protection applies. Through constitutional provision in 41 states and at the Federal level, utterances made in the course of speech or debate in legislative chambers, by members of lawmaking bodies, may not be questioned outside those precincts or made the subject of suit. In other words, floor discussion is absolutely privileged. This provision is rooted in the history of parliamentary bodies in

England, and derives from a policy of giving these houses a necessary degree of independence from possibly hostile executive and judicial branches. Also, matter, even defamatory, appearing in the published journals or proceedings of legislatures, is privileged against civil action.

With regard to liability, it has long been held that, while floor utterances are privileged, any defamatory matter spoken or published by a legislator outside the chamber or place of meeting, is subject to ordinary rules of law. A Congressman who attacked a citizen with libelous words outside the House of Representatives was made the defendant in a successful suit for damages. **James v. Powell**, 14 N.Y. 2d 881, 200 N.E. 2d 772 (1964).

What remained undecided was the impact of criminal law in the area of floor utterances by Congressmen, and by analogy, other legislators. A case of this sort was presented to the Supreme Court recently, involving the criminal conviction of a House member from Maryland who stood charged with receiving pay for making a speech in the House in defense of certain independent savings and loan associations. He was accused specifically of making the speech for pay as a result of a conspiracy to violate the Conflict of Interest statutes (18 U.S.C. Sec. 281, 371, 1964 ed.) and to deprive the Government of the benefit of his services unsullied by the taint of bribery and corruption. A related charge consisted of interceding with the Justice Department, for pay, to prevent criminal prosecution of certain of the Maryland savings and loan officials. After conviction at the trial level, the Court of Appeals reversed as regards the speech-for-pay charge, holding that the utterance of a Congressman on the floor of the House, and the circumstances surrounding it, even though possibly tainted with venality, may not be made the subject of criminal prosecution. As to the Justice Department portion of the indictment, retrial was authorized. Upon a writ of certiorari, the Supreme Court affirmed the Court of Appeals ruling. The Court said that the speech or debate clause of the Constitution (Art. 1, sec. 6) precludes judicial inquiry into the motivations for a Congressman's speech in the House chamber, and prevents such a speech from being made the basis of a criminal charge against the Member for conspiracy to defraud the Government by impeding the discharge of its functions. The policy of the privilege was based on the desire to protect the legislative branch against prosecution by a possibly hostile executive, and trial before a possibly unfriendly judiciary. The Supreme Court, moreover, said that the immunity extended not only to the content of the speech but to the surrounding circumstances, even though the conspiracy rather than the speech itself was the gravamen or basis of the charge. The case was remanded for retrial of its other aspects, purged of all allusions to the speech or matters concerning it. (In this case, upon retrial, the defendant was sentenced to prison. He had already lost his House seat at the polls after charges were brought). **U.S. v. Johnson**, 337 F. 2d 180 (1964), 383 U.S. 169 (1966). It should be pointed out that each of the Houses of Congress is, under the Constitution, the judge of the elections and qualifications of its members, and that it may expel a member by a two-thirds vote, as well as punish a member "for disorderly behaviour." These sanctions may have been felt sufficient by the Court to justify abstention by the judiciary from intruding into the discipline of a coordinate branch of government.

Chapter 7

RECENT DEVELOPMENTS IN
THE LAW OF OFFICERS

Relationship to Administrative Process

As government has become more complex and as its
functions have ramified, the traditional law governing public
officers has more and more merged into the general
law governing public administration in its larger sense. Vast
professional, highly trained, technically qualified, staffs now
perform the functions that a comparatively few elected or
appointed officials did only a few decades ago (and many
functions that were undreamed of within the recent memory
of many). Traditional ways of looking at the official's
relation to the public and to the agencies that employ him
have changed. Comparatively few persons, in relation to the
total force performing official functions, must now give bond
for the faithful performance of duty, possess an official
seal, take an oath of office, answer to quo warranto proceedings, be made subject to mandamus actions, and the
like. Because government has become so complex, the citizen
in dealing with it has come in many cases to feel that it
is bureaucratic in the derogatory sense, that its functionaries
no longer feel any concern for his particular needs and concerns, and that he is in many cases treated in a cavalier or
negligent manner. There has been a groping for ways by
which the citizen may cope with administrative monstrosity
and secure action, or remedy, from his government, in a
reasonably effective and expeditious manner.

Traditional Citizens' Remedies

1. "Write Your Congressman"
   The Congressman, particularly the Representative, and
his counterpart in the state legislatures, has long been re-

garded, and has regarded himself, as a sort of citizen's tribune. He gives, according to surveys and their findings, a large amount of his time and his staff's time to "case work" for his constituents. He helps them with crop and tax problems, with Veterans Administration claims, pension matters, Social Security, Medicare, military academy appointments and a host of other concerns. He sometimes serves as a go-between in finding government jobs, and as an opener of official doors and a cutter of leagues of red tape. However, his services are of necessity spotty and irregularly performed; a legislator securely in office, a committee chairman, one from a large populous constituency must necessarily give less of his time and effort to run-of-the-mill citizens' business than a man from a rural constituency, less entrenched in office, not burdened with committee business, and perhaps more eager to make a name for himself as an assiduous guardian of the common man's weal. Moreover, Congressional and legislative work of this kind is not coordinated; no pattern of agency abuse emerges from the sum total of service performed as it affects the workings of any particular department, since no one can analyze all of the mass of service performed as a whole. Hence the agencies themselves do not receive the benefit of an overall evaluation of their strengths and weaknesses as they serve their functions. An effort is usually made to handle "Congressional mail" with dispatch, but no net benefit inures to the ordinary citizen who does not use or cannot use his Congressman or legislator. The average legislator or junior Congressman does not possess the prestige or the political and administrative "know-how" to pull the right wires, or will only do so for a particularly influential constituent. Thus, some meritorious cases that do reach Congressmen and their state counterparts do not receive ultimate justice.

2. Agency Corrective Devices

Some agencies, some mayors and supervisors at various government levels, recognizing that the citizen often needs simple information and guidance rather than remedial action, have sought to provide this service by a variety of means. Trailers in cities go to neighborhoods remote from City

Hall. Displays, exhibits, information offices and pamphlets are brought into play in an effort to inform the citizen. Yet all too often those who most need the information and help do not receive, or do not know how to receive, it. Resentment against government, "the establishment," and "city hall," may develop where comparatively simple devices may forestall it.

3. Other Existing Devices

Various government agencies at the Federal level, and perhaps at the state and local level, correct some types of fiscal and administrative abuses, as part of their regular functions. The Budget Bureau and the General Accounting Office, in differing ways, serve as fiscal correctives and (particularly the latter) as watchdogs of internal lapses within Federal agencies in the area of financial management. These are not normally accessible to the ordinary citizen, however. They are not designed to serve his needs; at the most, they provide some assurance that obvious waste and misapplication of public funds will not long go concealed or unnoticed.

Proposed Remedies

1. Citzens' Review Boards

Particularly with regard to the police and peace officers, there has grown up in urban areas in recent years a feeling that the average citizen is abused and pushed around. Especially among the poor and minority groups, an attitude of hostility has grown up; it is felt that the normal means of bringing grievance actions within the offending agency will not only bring no effective correction but may excite reprisals. As the urban poor have attained a greater degree of organization, and a sense of latent and actual power, a demand has grown up for boards of review and correction that will be manned by those of their own number, with or without some representation from the agency involved. In any event, feeling rightly or wrongly that they cannot secure fairness from existing remedial machinery in the law enforcement agencies, members of these urban minorities have pressed for new methods of controlling and bringing to book the authorities they feel are oppressing them. In New York, Philadelphia, Syracuse, Rochester and other cities, this issue has been agitated, with varying degrees of success. Where boards of the citizen-review type have been set up, as in Philadelphia, the results do not as yet show conclusively whether they serve to alleviate the conditions complained of. The police, naturally, feel that such boards will hamstring effective law enforcement, undermine departmental morale and discipline, deter officers from courageously enforcing the law in areas of racial or ethnic tension, and make in the long run for a lower level of public safety. Only time and events will tell if these fears are well grounded. Ordinances setting up such boards generally provide that a citizen, alleging brutality or other misconduct on the part of an enforcement agency, may file a complaint with the board, which in turn is empowered to engage in fact finding operations, hold hearings, and endeavor to resolve the matter administratively. Various remedies provided depend on the extent of the power vested in the board. Some provide for bringing offending officers to trial, fining, demoting or in extreme cases discharging them and/or filing regular criminal charges against them. Other systems would provide for ascertaining the facts and making a report to the mayor or other proper official clothed with power to take final action.

2. The Ombudsman and Similar Proposals

Much interest, since 1960, has centered in this countr y on a device for redressing administrative complaints against public officials and agencies, which has had success in Scandinavian countries and in New Zealand. Since early in the last century, Sweden has had a public officer called an Ombudsman, who is given authority to receive complaints from citizens concerning all kinds of administrative and official mistakes and mistreatment. He has a staff with which he may make due investigation and study of the facts. In Sweden, if he finds lapses in the bureaucracy involved, he has the weapon of publicity through which he may focus attention on the offense and secure remedial action. The Ombudsman does not ordinarily possess power to administer correction himself, nor may he force an agency to act by direct means. His method is simply and basically to turn a spotlight of public attention on the offending bureau, publicizing its lapses, and to secure correction by this means. The Ombudsman exists in Norway, Denmark, Finland and New Zealand as well as in Sweden. The organization of the official's staff, and the degree of power vested in him, varies considerably. The Ombudsman may not reverse court decisions, nor may he intrude into legislative or executive discretion. He does not set or alter policy; he sees to it that existing policy is carried out, and that agencies adhere to their own procedures where these have been ignored, violated or evaded to the citizen's disadvantage. He may recommend procedural or policy changes. The effectiveness of the office rests in the amount of moral force it may exert, in its lack of hidden motive or axe-grinding, and in its freedom to pursue the ideal of justice without reference to internal agency politics or hierarchical considerations that so often hamstring efforts at effective corrective action within the bureaus themselves. The Ombudsman is beholden to nothing but the sovereignty that employs him and to the ideal of the public good. He is answerable to no superior bureaucrat, and his career is not affected by his actions so long as they center in the seeking of justice for the citizen. It is important to realize that the office affords no panacea by reason of its mere existence. The nations in which it has proved successful are lands with a high degree of citizen respect for law, with a highly developed merit system and civil service, with a tradition of orderly behavior, and with an educated citizenry that is to a considerable degree aware of its rights under law and procedure. The countries employing the Ombudsman are all small geographically, with a relatively homogeneous population. The official, either personally or by means of his staff, is able to travel about and receive complaints and gather grievances from the citizenry. In some cases there are branch offices easily accessible to the people. Parliamentary and executive officials, and the Crown where applicable, back the official and sustain his independence to seek and urge corrective action. The Ombudsman enjoys a high reputation for fairness with the agencies, and appropriate corrections and adjustments are generally forthcoming with a minimum of reluctance. Often, the decisions of a subordinate, perhaps based on a misinterpretation of applicable regulations within the agency, are to blame for the complaint. The office has one distinct advantage over Congressional or parliamentary service to constituents. Where the latter is haphazard, unfocused and contributory to little overall enlightenment as regards agency conduct and misconduct, the Ombudsman's office serves as a focal point for fact gathering. It quickly becomes apparent if complaints from citizens center in the actions of a few agencies or offices. It is readily seen if some law or administrative ruling gives rise to widespread misunderstanding or difficulty. The Ombudsman's functions, in short, bring quickly to light the areas of particular trouble and resentment or frustration in the governmental structure. Corrections in a comparatively few of these areas may result in a material lowering of popular discontent.

It remains to be seen whether such a device will work to advantage in a large, complex society, with great extremes between wealth and poverty, with wide gaps between education and illiteracy, and with traditions and norms at variance both with those of the Ombudsman countries and within itself. The New England town meeting has provided, in a small area of this country, an existing sense of citizen participation in local government; its counterpart survives today in many small rural areas throughout the land where citizens feel close to their government and to those who administer it. It is in the vast and faceless impersonal cities and metropolitan areas that the Ombudsman system or any imitation of it would meet its supreme test. With no respected, established, civil service tradition, with little popular regard for the institutions of government by any name designated, with a feeling (founded or unfounded) that government functions through officials at all levels who are "on the take," with no homogeneity of population and no common culture of rooted tradition, with a feeling among too many that laws are meant to be broken or evaded and not respected and obeyed—with all these handicaps, the Ombudsman or his analogue would be confronted in the resentful masses of the urban lower classes in the United States. The agencies with which he would have to deal, particularly at the local level, are in many instances case-hardened to receiving complaints and brushing them aside, and may be less amenable to the publicity weapon that works so well in the Ombudsman countries. Nevertheless, the concept of this office as a device for ameliorating governmental service to the citizen, defusing explosive situations, and generally raising both the level of service of, and popular attitudes toward, the institutions of government, has found wide interest. Articles and books have been written about it. One of the best is Walter Gellhorn's **When Americans Complain** (Harvard University Press, 1966). It is based on close observation of the office in operation in the named countries, on analyses of non-Ombudsman types of corrective or information agencies in other countries (France, Japan, Russia and others); and on possible applications and uses of the device in this country. That there is a need for some sort of bridge between citizen complaint and governmental action there is no doubt. Bills have been introduced in Congress to set up some sort of Administrative Counsel or similarly named office, clothing it with powers not greatly different from the more successful attributes of the Ombudsman. An act passed in 1964, to create an Administrative Conference of the United States, remains a dead letter as this book goes to press, by reason of the President's failure or inability to find an executive head and members of the administering board.* Obviously, its executive must have a rare combination of skills, personal characteristics and acumen to make a successful beginning. Probably the state and local governments will launch a successful operation of this kind before it becomes rooted at the Federal level.

---

*As this book was going to press, it was announced that President Johnson had named Professor Jerre S. Williams to head the Conference, and had named former Congressman Joe M. Kilgore and others to membership on the body.

Chapter 8

OF ROTTEN BOROUGHS, POLITICAL THICKETS, AND SLIDE-RULE SUFFRAGE

Legislative Apportionment in English and American History

In England, governmental history after 1215 reflected the gradual transition of power from an absolute monarch to an evolving form of parliamentary—that is, representative—government. At first, and for many centuries, the representation was not of the common people, but of the titled nobility, landed gentry, mercantile and financial interests, clergy, universities, established towns, counties, and boroughs, and other influential entities. A feudal pattern of representation and apportionment made the House of Commons (the "Mother of Parliaments") in no sense reflective of popular will, nor did it change significantly with the times. "Taxation without representation." applied, prior to 1832 and to some extent afterward, to many classes besides the colonial possessions. Particularly after the Industrial Revolution around 1800, the failure of Commons to respond to growing needs of a changing country became obvious, and increasingly irritating to large numbers of articulate and educated people. New industrial cities, such as Birmingham, Manchester, Sheffield, Leeds and Liverpool, grew up, possessed of no voice, or almost none, in the House of Commons. At the same time, old sections and boroughs, once influential, had become depopulated and continued to return members to the House. "Pocket boroughs" with power of representation belonged to the persons who by hereditary right held the land involved. These and other constituencies could be bartered, traded, bought and sold, with the right to return legislators included in the transaction. "Rotten boroughs," such as Old Sarum (with two representatives and no inhabitants), became glaring symbols of the anachronistic system of parliamentary apportionment.

An aroused and militant electorate, although with little voice in Parliament, was heard in the ministries. Their leaders, while to a great extent members of Parliament themselves, were sufficiently impressed with the need for reform to agitate the question during the 1820's and the early 1830's. Under the Prime Minister, Earl Gray, and with a strong Parliamentary leadership alive to the temper of the times, a reform measure was pressed under Whig Party sponsorship. Talk was rife of uprising and revolution, but actually the likelihood of armed conflict was slight. The bill that emerged was more oriented toward the aristocracy than toward universal representation as we understand it. It rectified the most glaring imbalances, however; and took some seats from extinct or over-represented constituencies and distributed them more equitably. After one dissolution of Parliament, much legislative maneuvering, the resignation of Grey and Lord Brougham and others, and their restoration to office, the bill was finally forced through the House of Lords only because the King promised the Prime Minister to create enough new peers to outvote the Lords' opposition. At last the bill was passed. What was demonstrated was that a parliamentary body, no matter how badly apportioned, no matter how many vested interests may oppose any change, can be forced by the weight of an aroused and militant electorate and political leadership to reform itself. (The significant action was the vote in the House of Commons. Here, the mal-apportioned body voted to change its own makeup). The great lesson of the Great Reform Bill of 1832 was lost on the United States. When segments of the American electorate found various legislative bodies obdurate and deaf to demands for change in apportionment patterns, they resorted not to continued political agitation, but turned to the judiciary. Courts and judges did not order the British Parliament to reform itself—the people and their leadership carried the day through the normal political processes.

In the early days in the United States, after Independence and the adoption of the Constitution, the legislatures of the various states contained two houses each, apportioned largely according to population. Each member was elected by a constituency approximately equal in numbers to others in the state. Efforts were made later, by interests opposing changes in mid-twentieth century patterns of apportionment, to show that historically one house of the legislature typically was based on a non-population pattern of representation. History does not bear out this contention. When the Northwest Ordinance was passed in 1787 (the year the Constitution of the United States was adopted), provision was made that legislatures to be set up in the new territories would have a population base for representation in both houses. ("A proportionate representation of the people in the legislature.") This is not to say, of course, that popular sovereignty or universal suffrage existed, or that imbalances were not prevalent. The vote was restricted to free white males, usually property owners, with at times other qualifications. New areas, and sections of the states that experienced later settlement and growth, felt discriminated against by reason of concentrations of legislative seats and political power in the older seaboard sections where wealth and property were centered.

The Constitution of the nation was, of course, itself the product of compromise on the representation issue. It became clear that the smaller states, having enjoyed equality in Congress with the larger ones under the Confederation, would not ratify a new organic document unless this equality were preserved. At the same time, the larger states were insistent that numbers of inhabitants be made the basis of representation in the legislative body. Each unit was a sovereignty; the purpose was to fuse them all into a new experimental nation—a federated republic, "a more perfect union." Compromise offered a way out. It was decided to have a two-house Congress, with a Senate composed of two members elected from each state, regardless of population; and a House of Representatives whose members "shall be apportioned among the several states which may be included within this union, according to their respective numbers. . ." A decennial census was provided for, to determine the population base for House membership and direct taxation. (Art. I, sec. 2). Section 4 of the Legislative Article gave to the state legislatures the power to prescribe "the times, places, and manner of holding elections for Senators and Representatives," but the Congress "may at any time by law make or alter such regulations. . ." Other provisions made each House "the judge of the elections, returns, and qualifications of its own members" and granted the Houses power to discipline and expel members. The Amendment Article (no. V) provided that "no state, without its consent, shall be deprived of its equal suffrage in the Senate." These provisions in the Federal Constitution provide all the guidance the organic law affords directly, concerning the makeup of the Houses of Congress, so far as membership allocation and apportionment is concerned. As to the states, references to an executive and a legislature of a state occur frequently; certain powers are conferred upon them with reference to election of Congress members and filling vacancies; the state legislatures, originally and up to 1913, elected the Senators; a "guaranty clause" provided that "the United States shall guarantee to every state in this union a republican form of government," and (most significantly in the light of apportionment cases to come) the Fourteenth Amendment secured to citizens of states and the United States certain "privileges and immunities," as well as a right to "due process of law" and "the equal protection of the laws." This amendment again stated that "Representatives shall be apportioned among the several States according to their respective numbers." Nothing in the Constitution says how Representatives shall be allotted or apportioned **within** the states, merely how the number of Representatives allocated **to** a state shall be determined. Each state shall have at least one Representative (Art. I, sec. 2), but otherwise all shall be apportioned to the states on a population basis.

At various times beginning with the middle of the last century and continuing, with lapses, to 1929, Congress attempted to specify by statute that the states should divide themselves into Congressional districts composed of compact and contiguous territory, and containing as nearly as feasible equal numbers of inhabitants. These laws were not enforced, nor would it have been practically or politically possible to enforce them. In the early period of our history, for perhaps fifty years, House members were generally elected at large. Districting has become the general method since perhaps 1840. In 1965, the House passed a bill to require all states with more than a single House member to use districts, each to be not more than 15 percent above or below the number of inhabitants in the state's average. Under the bill, one apportionment act may be passed after each census. The general practice now is that if a districted state receives an additional Representative because of population growth, it may elect the new one(s) at large, while the existing members run from their districts; or it may redistrict the whole state. If a state loses representation, it must redistrict; failing this, all the members must run from the state at large. Because most Congressmen with established districts prefer to run from them rather than from the state as a whole, generally a redistricting occurs. State legislatures, left without effective Congressional guidance, laid out districts with gross disparities in numbers of inhabitants. Normally, for many reasons rooted in history and grounded in the clash of interests reflected in the legislatures themselves, more lightly populated areas and rural sections enjoyed over-representation, while growing cities and metropolitan areas found themselves with many voters sharing few Congressmen. The state and Federal imbalances were intertwined, and for similar reasons.

Space will not permit elaborate treatment of the reasons for imbalance in the representation and apportionment structure, state and Federal. Suffice it to say that in the early days districts for state legislatures were approximately equal in population. Most original state constitutions required this. Population changes within states, shifts in economic and industrial patterns, the decline of agriculture as the basic source of wealth and of rural communities as the seat of the population, all contributed to a growing imbalance in the allocation of legislative seats. The size of districts, counties, towns, townships and other local units from which legislators were chosen, reflected these shifting patterns. For reasons of local pride, historical tradition, political ambition and anxiety over the possible consequences of change in legislative districting patterns, the legislators from the declining areas were reluctant to surrender the reins of power and turn them over to others from areas they considered alien and possibly hostile to their vital interests.

Moreover, political parties, having power bases grounded in existing legislative seats and constituencies, were often not amenable to changes that might throw control of the government into opposing hands. Even within a single party, a "rural faction" might feel apprehensive over the prospect of yielding power to an "urban faction." Visceral fears of urban "Bloc votes," terror of "big labor" and the "welfare vote" and the "spenders" who might saddle the state with bonded indebtedness that other more substantial interests would have to pay off, and fear of the Negro vote as more Negroes gravitated to urban centers—all these terrors and many others gave real or fancied grounds for vested rural and small-town interests to cling in desperation to disproportionate and unjustifiable power via legislative seats.

The consequences of all this were many. State legislatures, being increasingly unresponsive to demands for social and economic, fiscal, educational and other changes wanted by large segments of the people, declined in relative importance. Cities and metropolitan areas, and frustrated state executives, turned to the Federal Government for services and funds that would under a more equitable legislative structure have been forthcoming from the state. This further emphasized an already declining state role in national affairs, and contributed much to plaintive cries from the state capitals that they were being by-passed. Presidents, beginning with President Eisenhower in the 1950's, appointed commissions to study this problem and consider redressing the growing imbalance between the roles and services of state and Federal governments. A statutory Advisory Commission on Intergovernmental Relations has been formed, and is conducting studies in the area of cooperation between the governmental levels, and a possible rectifying of imbalances. However, so long as state legislatures reflected minority viewpoints and outmoded electoral bases, just so long would they lag in implementing and participating in the larger and more progressive trends in government service, particularly in service to larger population centers.

By 1960, most state legislatures contained two houses (only Nebraska has a single house) with one house at least theoretically based on a population foundation, and the other (generally the Senate) reflecting a county, town or other territorial base of representation. The "Federal analogy" was often invoked by spokesman for the status quo, to justify the election of one house on the basis of county or similar geographical constituency. The example of the United States Senate was cited, but without consideration of the fact that the states were not made up of sovereign counties, cities or towns, but of units set up only for reasons of governmental convenience, and revocable or changeable at will by the state government. Therefore, the need for the sort of compromise that dictated the composition of the Congress had no parallel in the states. The Senate with two members from each state was, as we have seen, the price of securing small-state ratification of the Constitution.

Litigation and Remedies

The door to corrective action at the legislative level, national and state, was effectively closed to those who would secure change in the unbalanced districting of state lawmaking bodies or the districts from which Congressmen were chosen, by the early 1960's. That is, it was closed to those who could not reason from the historical parallel of the Great Reform Act of England of 1832. To those who were too impatient to apply political heat, and the force of publicity and genuine leadership, to the recalcitrant legislators, there was a ready door open—the Federal judiciary. Why wait a half-century to secure reform by parliamentary means, as the English had done? Judicial activism, in a Supreme Court headed by Earl Warren, had already pointed a way to remedies in other difficult areas, such as school segregation. It would surely serve to open closed doors in the representation-apportionment area as well.

This had not always been the case. There was no established tradition at the Federal level, for the judiciary to intrude into political areas affecting the balance of power between coordinate branches of government, or the principle of separation of powers. There was little tendency among the state courts to grant relief in areas of this sort. Unhampered in many instances by a highly developed separation-of-powers doctrine as was the Federal judiciary, they would take jurisdiction of such questions, but would or could order little effective relief. In **Fergus** v. **Marks**, for example (321 Ill. 510, 152 N.E. 557 (1926)) the Illinois Supreme Court heard an apportionment case based upon an effort to force the legislature by mandamus to reapportion itself in compliance with a constitutional mandate, it having failed in that duty for a quarter-century. The court refused, saying that it was barred, as the arm of the judicial branch, from compelling a coordinate and coequal branch of government to take any action, even though the latter is under state constitutional requirement to act. The litigants must, in short, look to the very body that is guilty of inaction to secure action.

The Supreme Court of the United States received a later Illinois case, **Colegrove** v. **Green** (328 U.S. 549 (1946)), which invoked Federal jurisdiction based both on the Legislative Article and the due process and equal protection clauses of the Fourteenth Amendment. It had by now been 45 years since the Legislature had acted to reapportion itself. The High Court, with seven Justices participating and in a four-to-three decision, held that relief must be denied. Justice Frankfurter wrote the prevailing opinion (Justice Rutledge concurred separately) in which he pointed out that while the Court had jurisdiction, the matter was not "justiciable" by the Federal courts. It was of "peculiarly political nature" and the courts "ought not to enter this political thicket." "The remedy for unfairness," he said, "is to secure State legislatures that will apportion properly, or to invoke the ample powers of Congress." Justice Rutledge, concurring, felt that relief should not be denied on the ground of non-justiciability, but of abstention, pointing out that Congressional elections would be shortly forthcoming. The dissenters, speaking through Justice Black, felt that the matter was meet for adjudication, that the right to cast an equal ballot is one the courts should protect and vindicate, even through "political." Later cases showed deference to the Frankfurter opinion; although the court was divided, this ruling was to set the tone for Federal court inactivity until 1962.

In the latter year, the Court decided the case of **Baker v. Carr** (369 U. S. 186). The factual basis, and grounds for invoking the Court's assistance, were parallel to the **Colegrove** situation: the Tennessee legislature had failed, since 1901, to apportion itself despite a state constitutional requirement that it do so. The Tennessee state courts had refused to grant relief on grounds similar to those of the Illinois court. The governor had pleaded in vain with the legislature. The litigants, representing urban counties that suffered dilution of their votes in choosing legislators vis-a-vis rural counties, sought relief from a statutory three-judge Federal district court. Relief was denied on the precedent of the **Colegrove** case, and direct appeal was had to the Supreme Court. The lower court expressed uncertainty as to whether the case was properly "justiciable" because of the inconclusiveness of the opinions in the 1946 case. The Supreme Court majority in the **Baker** case, speaking through Justice Brennan, held affirmatively on the three key issues before it: that the appellants had standing to come to the Supreme Court, the Court had jurisdiction, and that the subject matter was meet for adjudication ("justiciable"). The reasoning employed by Justice Brennan in reaching his conclusions has been criticized by lawyers, judges and political scientists; but all the Court except two dissenters held that the matter was proper for adjudication by the Federal courts. The landmark nature of this decision may be inferred from the fact that the Court heard argument during both the 1960 and 1961 terms before reaching a decision. The six separate opinions in this one case comprise over 165 printed pages of text—perhaps one and six-tenths the size of this little book. For the first time a Federal court precedent was set: that state legislative districting and apportionment questions presented constitutional issues that were subject to judicial scrutiny and amenable to the award of appropriate and effective relief.

The relief sought in the leading case was not granted by the Supreme Court. The Court merely ordered the matter remanded to the Federal District Court where constitutionality would be determined and proper relief would be fashioned, if found needed. Critics have faulted the Supreme Court for not prescribing guidelines or indicators to assist the lower courts in this task. It would have been difficult for the High Court to do this, however, because of the multiplicity of fact situations and degrees of imbalance that would arise in different cases. In some cases, political remedies are more appropriate; some states have the initiative and referendum and other devices that could be brought into play. Some states have constitutional provisions whereby their own courts may participate effectively in the apportioning process (Oregon and Arkansas are examples). At this early stage, the Court did not even pronounce on the desirability or constitutionality of having the same or differing population bases for a bicameral legislature.

The dissenting opinion should not be overlooked. Speaking for himself and Justice Harlan, Frankfurter took the same position he had taken in the **Colegrove** case, but phrased it far more eloquently and trenchantly. In one of his greatest opinions (and the last major one before illness forced him to retire), he warned of the manifold dangers facing the Court and the judiciary generally as they entered the arena of political controversy. One of the great strengths of the Court, he felt, was its detachment from, and aloofness from, the tug-of-war of the active political process. Its prestige derived to a great degree from this aloofness; this would be imperiled, and popular regard for the Court as an institution be eroded, by reason of political involvement. Moreover, he said that it is a mistake for persons to feel they can come running to the Court for a remedy or relief from every civil ill. "There is not under our Constitution a judicial remedy for every political mischief, for every undesirable exercise of legislative power. The Framers carefully and with deliberate forethought refused so to enthrone the judiciary. In this situation, as in others of like nature, appeal for relief does not belong here. Appeal must be to an informed, civically militant electorate. In a democratic society like ours, relief must come through an aroused popular conscience that sears the conscience of the people's representatives."

Few cases have had so immediate and drastic an effect as **Baker** v. **Carr**. Within a few weeks and months, courts were handing down various rulings bearing on legislative apportionment in many states; both the Federal and the state judiciary participated. Interim and permanent plans for redressing apportionment imbalances were devised to meet differing local and state situations. Later the same year, the Supreme Court invalidated the "county unit" system of voting by rurally-weighted balloting in Georgia party primaries.

Congressional Districting

The next major field for Supreme Court corrective action was that concerning districts for House of Representatives elections. As we have seen, the Constitution provided that the manner of electing members to the Senate and House rested with the state legislatures; Congress has the power to make or alter such regulations. Early in 1964, the Court decided the case of **Wesberry** v. **Sanders** (376 U. S. 1), in which it held "construed in its historical context, the command of Art. 1, § 2 that Representatives shall be chosen 'by the people of the several states' means that as nearly as practicable one man's vote in a congressional election is to be worth as much as another's." The litigants before the Court were from the Atlanta area, and claimed that they were subjected to deprivation of equal protection of the laws and other rights secured by the Constitution, by reason of the fact that the Fifth Georgia District, in which they lived and voted, had 823,680 inhabitants under the 1960 census, while the Ninth District of the same state had only 272,154, and the state's average district had 394,312. The district had been set up by a 1931 statute, and had not been changed since. Their action had been dismissed by a lower Federal court on the ground that this claim also presented a nonjusticiable "political question." The hardest matter to resolve in a Congressional districting case is the extent and possible exclusiveness of the power conferred upon Congress to govern elections to the House, in Art. I, sec. 4 of the Constitution. Justice Frankfurter's view, that this power rests with Congress exclusively, was repudiated by the Court, in Justice Black's majority opinion in the **Wesberry** case. The Court had jurisdiction and power to grant relief in cases where a state districting statute had the effect of debasing a citizen's right to vote by reason of delineating districts with extreme disparities of population.

If a state allows its Congressmen to run at large, the effect is automatically to give each ballot counted an equal weight with each other ballot. It would be unfair and illogical to permit districts to stand, if population disparities make a vote in one district carry materially more weight than a vote in another district. Absolute mathematical precision is not possible and is not demanded, but the goal should none the less be "one person, one vote." Again, the case was remanded to the lower court for further action and the formulation of specific relief. Two justices dissented in toto, and one in part, from the majority decision. Justice Harlan emphasized two points: that the subject matter in these cases is not properly meet for judicial determination; and that the Constitution in the Legislative Article had conferred exclusive power upon the states and upon Congress to regulate such matters as Congressional districting in the States. Justice Harlan felt the majority's decision reflected a lack of confidence that Congress would act, and held it to be a violation of the separation of powers doctrine. Also, he felt that continued court intervention into these areas would weaken the political process and encourage popular inertia in such matters, through leading citizens to feel that no matter how little they did to improve matters, the courts would always stand ready to provide a corrective remedy whenever wanted.

Finally, in **Reynolds** v. **Sims** (377 U. S. 533), decided in June 1964, the Court was called upon to ascertain "whether there are any constitutionally cognizable principles which would justify departures from the basic standard of equality among voters in the apportionment of seats in state legislatures." Invalidating apportionment plans in six specific states, the Court (Chief Justice Warren writing the majority opinion) held that "both houses of a state legislature must be apportioned on a population basis. . .the Equal Protection

Clause requires that a state make an honest and good faith effort to construct districts, in both houses of its legislature, as nearly of equal population as is practicable.'' Lower courts were again left to work out specific plans for particular state situations. Population was to be the controlling criterion, and any departures must reflect some rational basis and not a purpose of invidious discrimination. States were specifically not permitted to structure one house of the legislature on a geographic basis; the ''Federal analogy'' was held to be inapposite to the relationship prevailing between the states and their political subdivisions.

A case involving Colorado, decided the same day, proved to be the most extreme of the group. Here, the people of the state, voting in a statewide initiative petition, on a ''one man-one vote'' basis, with urban and rural voters in agreement, had approved a districting plan under which the House would be based on population and the Senate on a modified but fair geographic-population formula. The voters of Colorado had specifically, on the same day, rejected an apportionment formula that would have placed both houses on a population basis. Nevertheless, this plan, based on a rational state policy, was sent down the drain with all the rest. The reason? Chief Justice Warren's ipse dixit that ''an individual's constitutionally protected right to cast an equally weighted vote cannot be denied even by a vote of a majority of a state's electorate'' if what the Court calls the ''requirements of the Equal Protection Clause'' are not met. The Stewart-Clark dissent demolished the weak reasoning in the Warren opinion. Groups and interests, as well as people, are to be considered. Geography and topography have significance in the apportionment pattern. No one's right to vote has been denied, impaired or restricted in any of these cases. The cases have nothing to do with the weighting or diluting of votes in any district. The majority simply took one philosophical doctrine, among a number of equally valid and applicable ones, and elevated it to the standing of a constitutional rule, forcing it on all the states alike, without regard to individual history, geography, heritage and distribution of population. ''The Court says that the requirements of the

Equal Protection Clause can be met in any state only by the uncritical, simplistic and heavy-handed application of sixth-grade arithmetic." (**Lucas** v. **44th General Assembly of Colorado**, 377 U. S. 713 (1964)).

Reapportionment Postscript

Efforts at compliance with the Supreme Court's majority holdings have been made in most of the states. Sometimes these have been made under Federal court prodding, sometimes by state court order or pressure, sometimes by legislative action independent of court direction (although with the threat of it ever present). Adverse press and public reaction proved to be less vehement than many had anticipated. Movements to overturn the apportionment decisions centered basically in two efforts:

(1) To enact Congressional legislation withdrawing from the Supreme Court the power to hear representation-apportionment cases involving state legislatures (under the Constitutional power of Congress to regulate the appellate jurisdiction of the Court); and

(2) To amend the Constitution so as to permit any state with a bicameral legislature to take factors other than population into account in apportioning one of the houses.

Time moved too fast for the opponents, and the surprisingly mild popular reaction to these decisions left little power base for strong opposition. The withdrawal-of-jurisdiction bill (the Tuck bill) was passed by the House in Auguat 1964 by a vote of 218 to 175. This bill never was seriously considered by the Senate. The amendment effort reached its high water mark in August 1965, when the Senate voted 57 to 39 in favor of the amendment. This was only seven votes short of the two-thirds needed to propose the amendment. However, after these votes, the power of the opposition receded. As was to be expected, a new vested interest had appeared. The state legislatures that had been elected pursuant to the reapportionment decrees, and a House of Representatives reflective of new and egalitarian districts, would be little disposed to vote any measure that would have tended to restore the old status quo, even in part. The Court had enthroned a new ruling class. What the benefits of this quiet and bloodless revolution will be for the states and for the nation, no one may predict with certainty yet. The stability of the suburban areas that stand to benefit the most from the reapportionments augurs well for the view that the long-range results will be beneficial for the political structure and for the country as a whole.

Gerrymandering and Gomillion

The technique of the gerrymander (the practice of drawing electoral district lines so as to favor one party and confine or "waste" the votes of another) has a long history in this country, and is assiduously practiced to this day. The courts have been reluctant to intervene in these truly "political questions" because of the difficulty of establishing, in a fact situation, that a true gerrymander has occurred, and of fashioning appropriate judicial relief. Only when racial discrimination has been charged has the Supreme Court generally taken notice of these cases, and the results have been mixed. In **Wright** v. **Rockefeller** (376 U. S. 54 (1964)); the Court found no basis for the claim that a Manhattan Congressional district in New York was gerrymandered to concentrate Negro voters in one district. The districts were close to an equal basis of population, and residential patterns tended to concentrate Negroes in one of the areas. However, in **Gomillion** v. **Lightfoot** (364 U. S. 347), decided in 1960, the Court found that a conscious and deliberate effort had been made to redraw the city boundaries of Tuskeegee, Alabama, so as to fence Negro residents outside the city limits and into the surrounding county (Macon) where the preponderant white electorate would neutralize their votes. The intent of the effort here was clear: a many-sided boundary had been carefully drawn to define the district involved. The particular gerrymander was invalidated, but the Court was careful to indicate its reluctance to enter the field of gerrymandering generally. It would appear that only some policy consideration such as a civil rights or race issue would lead the Court into this area of controversy.

100

BIBLIOGRAPHY

Alexander, Herbert E., **Regulation of Political Finance**, Berkeley, University of California Institute of Governmental Studies, 1966.

American Assembly, Columbia University, **State Legislatures in American Politics**. Englewood Cliffs, N. J., Prentice-Hall, 1966.

American Bar Association, Commission on Electoral College Reform, **Electing the President, A Report**, Chicago, The Association, 1967.

American Jurisprudence, vols. 42-43, **Public Officers**, secs. 1-520, San Francisco, Bancroft-Whitney Co., 1942 (suppl. to 1967).

Anderson, Walter H., **A Treatise on the Law of Sheriffs, Coroners and Constables, with forms**. Perm. ed., Buffalo, N. Y., Dennis & Co., 1947.

Association of the Bar of the City of New York, Special Committee on the Federal Conflict of Interest Laws, **Conflict of Interest in the Federal Service**, Cambridge, Mass., Harvard Univ. Press, 1960.

Baker, Gordon E., **The Reapportionment Revolution**, New York, Random House, 1966.

Bertelsman, W. O., "Libel and Public Men," 52 **American Bar Association Journal** 657 (1966).

Blair, George S., **American Legislatures: Structure and Process**, New York, Harper & Row, 1967.

Chicago, University, Law School, **Conference on Conflict of Interest, Feb. 20, 1961**. (Conference series, no. 17)

Clapp, Charles L., **The Congressman, His Work as He Sees It**, Washington, Brookings Institution, 1963.

"Conflicts of Interest, A Symposium," 24 **Federal Bar Journal**, no. 3 (summer 1964).

Cummings, C. Milton, ed., **The National Elections of 1964**, Washington, Brookings Institution, 1966.

Danelski, David J., **A Supreme Court Justice is Appointed**, New York, Random House, 1964.

Deakin, James, **The Lobbyists**, Washington, Public Affairs Press, 1966.

De Grazia, Alfred, ed., **Congress, The First Branch of Government, Twelve Studies**, Washington, American Enterprise Institute, 1966.

Dixon, Robert G., Jr., "Legislative Apportionment and the Federal Constitution," 27 **Law & Contemporary Problems** 329 (1962).

"The Ethical Lawyer and Governmental Influence," 12 **Virginia Law Weekly, Dicta Comp.** (1961).

Evins, Joe L., **Understanding Congress**, New York, Clarkson N. Potter, Inc., 1963.

Fesler, James W., ed., **The 50 States and Their Local Governments**, New York, Alfred A. Knopf, 1967.

Fordham, Jefferson B., **The State Legislative Institution**, Philadelphia, Univ. of Pennsylvania Press, 1959.

Gellhorn, Walter, **When Americans Complain**, Cambridge, Mass., Harvard Univ. Press, 1966.

Graves, W. Brooke, **American Intergovernmental Relations**, New York, Chas. Scribner's Sons, 1964.

Greene, Lee S., ed., **City Bosses and Political Machines** (353 Annals of the American Academy of Political and Social Science, May 1964).

Griffith, Ernest S., **Congress, Its Contemporary Role**, 4th ed., New York, New York Univ. Press, 1967.

Hart, James, **An Introduction to Administrative Law**, New York, F. S. Crofts, 1940.

Holtzman, Abraham, **Interest Groups and Lobbying**, New York, Macmillan Co., 1966.

Horsky, Charles A., **The Washington Lawyer**, Boston, Little, Brown & Co., 1952.

Jennings, M. Kent (and L. H. Zeigler), eds., **The Electoral Process**, Englewood Cliffs, N. J., Prentice-Hall, 1966.

Keefe, William J. (and M. S. Ogul), **The American Legislative Process: Congress and the States**, Englewood Cliffs, N. J., Prentice-Hall, 1964.

Key, V. O., Jr., **Politics, Parties and Pressure Groups**, 5th ed., New York, Thos. Y. Crowell Co., 1964.

Koenig, Louis W., **The Chief Executive**, New York, Harcourt, Brace & World, 1964.

Lorch, Robert S., "Administrative Court via the Independent Hearing Officer," 51 **Judicature** 112 (1967).

McQuillin, Eugene, **The Law of Municipal Corporations**, 3d ed., 1968 rev. vol. 17 (Latta, ed.) Chicago, Callaghan & Co., 1968.

Minow, Newton N., **Equal Time**, New York, Atheneum, 1964.

Mitau, G. Theodore, **State and Local Government: Politics and Processes**, New York, Chas. Scribner's Sons, 1966.

Nickel, Henry V., "The New York Times Rule and Society's Interest in Providing a Redress for Defamatory Statements," 36 **George Washington Law Review** 424 (1967).

Philos, Conrad D., "The Conflict in Conflicts of Interest: The Rule of Law—The Role of Ethics," 27 **Federal Bar Journal** 7 (1967).

Ray, Verne M., ed., **Interpreting FCC Broadcast Rules & Regulations**, Thurmont, Md., TAB Books, 1966.

Salomon, Leon L., ed., **The Independent Federal Regulatory Agencies**, New York, H. W. Wilson Co., 1959.

Smith, C. E., **Voting and Election Laws: Laws for Voters**, Dobbs Ferry, N. Y., Oceana Publications, 1961.

Swenson, Rinehart J., **Federal Administrative Law**, New York, Ronald Press Co., 1952.

Todd, Alden L., **Justice on Trial: The Case of Louis D. Brandeis**, New York, McGraw-Hill, 1964.

U. S. Congress, House, Committee on the Judiciary, **Federal Conflict of Interest Legislation, Hearings**. . .Washington, U. S. Govt. Print. Off., 1960.

U. S. Congress, Senate, Committee on the Judiciary, **Ombudsman, Hearing**. . .Washington, U. S. Govt. Print. Off., 1966.

U. S. Congress, Senate, Library, **Factual Campaign Information**, Washington, U.S. Govt. Print. Off., 1968.

U. S., Library of Congress, Legislative Reference Service, **Election Law Guidebook**, Washington, U. S. Govt. Print. Off., 1968.

U. S. President's Commission on Campaign Costs, **Financing Presidential Campaigns: Report**, Washington, U. S. Govt. Print. Off., 1962.

U. S. President's Commission on Campaign Costs, **Legislative Recommendations, Transmitted**. . .**to the Congress, May 29, 1962**, Washington, U. S. Govt. Print. Off., 1962.

APPENDIX

Selected Federal statutes governing or affecting public employees and officials in connection with political activity are presented here. Included are the Federal Corrupt Practices Act, Title 2, U.S. Code, sections 241-256; the Federal Regulation of Lobbying Act, Title 2, U.S. Code, sections 261-270; and the principal portions of the Hatch Political Activities Act, Title 5, U.S. Code, sections 1501-1508 (applying to state and local employees) and sections 7321-7327 (applying to Federal employees). Particularly in relation to the Hatch Act, it is important to note that "public officials" are defined by Congress in differing ways for various purposes, and an officer or employee will need to scrutinize the act carefully to see if a given practice or activity of a political nature is permissible for him. The severity of the penalties imposed for violations makes it imperative that the act's coverage in a given instance be investigated before any activities of a political or semi-political nature are undertaken.

TITLE 2, U.S. CODE
FEDERAL CORRUPT PRACTICES

Section 241. Definitions.—When used in this title—

(a) The term "election" includes a general or special election, and, in the case of a Resident Commissioner from the Philippine Islands, an election by the Philippine Legislature, but does not include a primary election or convention of a political party;

(b) The term "candidate" means an individual whose name is presented at an election for election as Senator or Representative in, or Delegate or Resident Commissioner to, the Congress of the United States, whether or not such individual is elected;

(c) The term "political committee" includes any committee, association, or organization which accepts contributions or makes expenditures for the purpose of influencing or attempting to influence the election of candidates or presidential and vice presidential electors (1) in two or more States, or (2) whether or not in more than one State if such committee, association, or organization (other than a duly organized State or local committee of a political party) is a branch or subsidiary of a national committee, association, or organization;

(d) The term "contribution" includes a gift, subscription, loan, advance, or deposit, of money, or anything of value, and includes a contract, promise, or agreement, whether or not legally enforceable to make a contribution;

(e) The term "expenditure" includes a payment, distribution, loan, advance, deposit, or gift of money, or any thing of value, and includes a contract, promise, or agreement, whether or not legally enforceable, to make an expenditure;

(f) The term "person" includes an individual, partnership, committee, association, corporation, and any other organization, or group of persons;

(g) The term "Clerk" means the Clerk of the House of Representatives of the United States;

(h) The term "Secretary" means the Secretary of the Senate of the United States;

(i) The term "State" includes Territory and possession of the United States, (Feb. 28, 1925, c. 368, Title III, sec./ 302, 43 Stat. 1070.)

242. Chairman and treasurer of political committee—Duties as to contributions—Accounts and receipts— (a) Every political committee shall have a chairman and a treasurer. No contribution shall be accepted, and no expenditure made, by or on behalf of a political committee for the purpose of influencing an election until such chairman and treasurer have been chosen.

(b) It shall be the duty of the treasurer of a political committee to keep a detailed and exact account of—

(1) All contributions made to or for such committee;

(2) The name and address of every person making any such contribution, and the date thereof;

(3) All expenditures made by or on behalf of such committee; and

(4) The name and address of every person to whom any such expenditure is made, and the date thereof.

(c) It shall be the duty of the treasurer to obtain and keep a receipted bill, stating the particulars, for every expenditure by or on behalf of a political committee exceeding $10 in amount. The treasurer shall preserve all receipted bills and accounts required to be kept by this section for a period of at least two years from the date of the filing of the statement containing such items. (Feb. 28, 1925, c. 368, Title III, sec./ 303, 43 Stat. 1071.)

243. Accounts of contributions received.—Every person who receives a contribution for a political committee shall, on demand of the treasurer, and in any event within five days after the receipt of such contribution, render to the treasurer a detailed account thereof, including the name and address of the person making such contribution, and the date on which received (Feb. 28, 1925, c. 368, Title III, sec./ 304, 43 Stat. 1071.)

244. Statements by treasurer filed with Clerk of House of Representatives.—(a) The treasurer of a political committee shall file with the Clerk between the 1st and 10th days of March, June, and September, in each year, and also between the 10th and 15th days, and on the 5th day, next preceding the date on which a general election is to be held, at which candidates are to be elected in two or more States, and also on the 1st day of January, a statement containing, complete as of the day next preceding the date of filing—

(1) The name and address of each person who has made a contribution to or for such committee in one or more items of the aggregate amount or value, within the calendar year, of $100 or more, together with the amount and date of such contribution;

(2) The total sum of the contributions made to or for such committee during the calendar year and not stated under paragraph (1);

(3) The total sum of all contributions made to or for such committee during the calendar year;

(4) The name and address of each person to whom an expenditure in one or more items of the aggregate amount or value, within the calendar year, of $10 or more has been made by or on behalf of such committee, and the amount, date, and purpose of such expenditure;

(5) The total sum of all expenditures made by or on behalf of such committee during the calendar year and not stated under paragraph (4);

(6) The total sum of expenditures made by or on behalf of such committee during the calendar year.

(b) The statements required to be filed by subdivision (a) shall be cumulative during the calendar year to which they relate, but where there has been no change in an item reported in a previous statement only the amount need be carried forward.

(c) The statement filed on the 1st day of January shall cover the preceding calendar year. (Feb. 28, 1925, c. 368, Title III, sec./ 305, 43 Stat. 1071.)

245. Statements by others than political committee filed with Clerk of House of Representatives.—Every person (other than a political committee) who makes an expenditure in one or more items, other than by contribution to a political committee, aggregating $50 or more within a calendar year for the purpose of influencing in two or more States the election of candidates, shall file with the Clerk an itemized detailed statement of such expenditure in the same manner as required of the treasurer of a political committee by section 305 sec./ 244 of this title). (Feb. 28, 1925, c. 368, Title III, sec./ 306, 43 Stat. 1072.)

246. Statements by candidates for Senator, Representative, Delegate, or Resident Commissioner filed with Secretary of Senate and Clerk of House of Representatives.—(a) Every candidate for Senator shall file with the Secretary and every candidate for Representative, Delegate, or Resident Commissioner shall file with the Clerk not less than ten nor more than fifteen days before, and also within thirty days after, the date on which an election is to be held, a statement containing, complete as of the day next preceding the date of filing—

(1) A correct and itemized account of each contribution received by him or by any person for him with his knowledge or consent, from any source, in aid or support of his candidacy for election, or for the purpose of influencing the result of the election, together with the name of the person who has made such contribution;

(2) A correct and itemized account of each expenditure made by him or by any person for him with his knowledge or consent, in aid or support of his candidacy for election, or for the purpose of influencing the result of the election, together with the name of the person to whom such expenditure was made; except that only the total sum of expenditures for items specified in subdivision (c) of section 309 sec./ 248 of this title) need be stated:

(3) A statement of every promise or pledge made by him or by any person for him with his consent, prior to the closing of the polls on the day of the election, relative to the appointment or recommendation for appointment of any person to any public or private position or employment for the purpose of procuring support in his candidacy, and the name, address, and occupation of every person to whom any such promise or pledge has been made, together with the description of any such position. If no such promise or pledge has been made, that fact shall be specifically stated.

(b) The statements required to be filed by subdivision (a) shall be cumulative, but where there has been no change in an item reported in a previous statement only the amount need be carried forward.

(c) Every candidate shall inclose with his first statement a report, based upon the records of the proper State official, stating the total number of votes cast for all candidates for the office which the candidate seeks, at the general election next preceding the election at which he is a candidate. (Feb. 28, 1925, c. 368, Title III, para. 307, 43 Stat. 1072.)

247. Statements—Verification—Filing — Preservation — Inspection.—A statement required by this title to be filed by a candidate or treasurer of a political committee or other person with the Clerk or Secretary, as the case may be—

(a) Shall be verified by the oath or affirmation of the person filing such statement, taken before any officer authorized to administer oaths.

(b) Shall be deeemed properly filed when deposited in an established post office within the prescribed time, duly stamped, registered, and directed to the Clerk or Secretary at Washington, District of Columbia, but in the event it is not received, a duplicate of such statement shall be promptly filed upon notice, by the Clerk or Secretary of its nonreceipt;

(c) Shall be preserved by the Clerk or Secretary for a period of two years from the date of filing, shall constitute a part of the public records of his office, and shall be open to public inspection. (Feb. 28, 1925, c. 368, Title III, para. 308, 43 Stat. 1072.)

248. Limitation upon amount of expenditures by candiate.—(a) A candidate, in his campaign for election, shall not make expenditures in excess of the amount which he may lawfully make under the laws of the State in which he is a candidate, nor in excess of the amount which he may lawfully make under the provisions of this title.

(b) Unless the laws of his State prescribe a less amount as the maximum limit of campaign expenditures, a candidate may make expenditures up to—

(1) The sum of $10,000 if a candidate for Senator, or the sum of $2,500 if a candidate for Representative, Delegate, or Resident Commissioner; or

(2) An amount equal to the amount obtained by multiplying three cents by the total number of votes cast at the last general election for all candidates for the office which the candidate seeks, but in no event

exceeding $25,000 if a candidate for Senator or $5,000 if a candidate for Representative, Delegate, or Resident Commissioner.

(c) Money expended by a candidate to meet and discharge any assessment, fee, or charge made or levied upon candidate by the laws of the State in which he resides, or expended for his necessary personal, traveling, or subsistence expenses, or for stationery, postage, writing, or printing (other nan for use on billboards or in newspapers), for distributing letters, circulars, or posters, or for telegraph or telephone service, shall not be included in determining whether his expenditures have exceeded the sum fixed by paragraph (1) or (2) of subdivision (b) as the limit of campaign expenses of a candidate. (Feb. 28, 1925, c. 368, Title III, para. 309, 43 Stat. 1073.)

252. General penalties for violations.—(a) Any person who violates any of the foregoing provisions of this title, except those for which a specific penalty is imposed by sections 312 and 313, shall be fined not more than $1,000 or imprisoned not more than one year, or both.

(b) Any person who wilfully violates any of the foregoing provisions of this title, except those for which a specific penalty is imposed by sections 312 and 313, shall be fined not more than $10,000 and imprisoned not more than two years. (Feb. 28, 1925, c. 368, Title III, sec./ 314, 43 Stat. 1074.)

253. Expenses of election contests,—This title shall not limit or affect the right of any person to make expenditures for proper legal expenses in contesting the results of an election. (Feb. 28, 1925, c. 368, Title III, sec./ 315, 43 Stat. 1074.)

254. State laws not affected.—This title shall not be construed to annul the laws of any State relating to the nomination or election of candidates, unless directly inconsistent with the provisions of this title, or to exempt any candidate from complying with such State laws. (Feb. 28, 1925, c. 368, Title III, sec./ 316, 43 Stat. 1074.)

255. Partial invalidity.—If any provision of this title or the application thereof to any person or circumstance is held invalid, the validity of the remainder of the Act and of the application of such provision to other persons and circumstances shall not be affected thereby. (Feb. 28, 1925, c. 368, Title III, sec./ 317, 43 Stat. 1074.)

256. Short title.—This title may be cited as the "Federal Corrupt Practices Act, 1925." (Feb. 28, 1925, c. 368, Title III, sec./301, 43 Stat. 1070.)

REGULATION OF LOBBYING

Section 261. Definitions.—When used in this title | sec./ 261 and note-270 of this title| —

(a) The term "contribution" includes a gift, subscription, loan, advance, or deposit of money or anything of value and includes a contract, promise, or agreement, whether or not legally enforceable, to make a contribution.

(b) The term "expenditure" includes a payment, distribution, loan, advance, deposit, or gift of money or anything of value, and includes a contract, promise, or agreement, whether or not legally enforceable, to make an expenditure.

(c) The term "person" includes an individual, partnership, committee, association, corporation, and any other organization or group of persons.

(d) The term "Clerk" means the Clerk of the House of Representatives of the United States.

(e) The term "legislation" means bills, resolutions, amendments, nom-inations, and other matters pending or proposed in either House of Congress, and includes any other matter which may be the subject of action by either House. (Aug. 2, 1946, c. 753, Title III, sec./ 302, 60 Stat. 839.)

Short title.—Section 301 of Act Aug. 2, 1946, cited to text, provided: "This title | sec./ 261-270 of this title| may be cited as the "Federal Regulation of Lobbying Act.' "

262. Detailed accounts of contributions.—(a) It shall be the duty of every person who shall in any manner solicit or receive a contribution to any organization or fund for the purposes hereinafter |in para. 266 of this title| designated to keep a detailed and exact account of—

(1) all contributions of any amount or of any value whatsoever;

(2) the name and address of every person making any such contribution of $500 or more and the date thereof;

(3) all expenditures made by or on behalf of such organization or fund; and

(4) the name and address of every person to whom any such expenditure is made and the date thereof.

(b) It shall be the duty of such person to obtain and keep a receipted bill, stating the particulars, for every expenditure of such funds exceeding $10 in amount, and to preserve all receipted bills and accounts required to be kept by this section for a period of at least two years from the date of the filing of the statement containing such items. (Aug. 2, 1946, c. 753, Title III, para. 303, 60 Stat. 840.)

263. Receipts for contributions.— Every individual who receives a contribution of $500 or more for any of the purposes hereinafter |in para. 266 of this title| designated shall within five days after receipt thereof |render| to the person or organization for which such contribution was received a detailed account thereof, including the name and address of the person making such contribution and the date on which received. (Aug. 2, 1946, c. 753, Title III, para. 304, 60 Stat. 840.)

264. Statements to be filed with Clerk of House.—(a) Every person receiving any contributions or expending any money for the purposes designated in subparagraph (a) or (b) of section 307 |para. 266 (a), (b) of this title| shall file with the Clerk between the first and tenth day of each calendar quarter, a statement containing complete as of the day next preceding the date of filing—

(1) The name and address of each person who has made a contribution of $500 or more not mentioned in the preceding report; except that the first report filed pursuant to this title |para. 261-270 of this title| shall contain the name and address of each person who has made any contribution of $500 or more to such person since the effective date of this title |Aug. 2, 1946|;

(2) the total sum of the contributions made to or for such person during the calendar year and not stated under paragraph (1);

(3) the total sum of all contributions made to or for such person during the calendar year;

(4) the name and address of each person to whom an expenditure in one or more items of the aggregate amount or value, within the calendar year, of $10 or more has been made by or on behalf of such person, and the amount, date, and purpose of such expenditure;

(5) the total sum of all expenditures made by or on behalf of such person during the calendar year and not stated under paragraph (4);

(6) the total sum of expenditures made by or on behalf of such person during the calendar year.

(b) The statements required to be filed by subsection (a) shall be cumulative during the calendar year to which they relate, but where there has been no change in an item reported in a previous statement only the amount need be carried forward. (Aug. 2, 1946, c. 753, Title III, para. 305, 60 Stat. 840.)

265. Statement preserved for two years.—A statement required by this title |para. 261-270 of this title| to be filed with the Clerk—

(a) shall be deemed properly filed when deposited in an established post office within the prescribed time, duly stamped, registered, and directed to the Clerk of the House of Representatives of the United States, Washington, District of Columbia, but in the event it is not received, a duplicate of such statement shall be promptly filed upon notice by the Clerk of its nonreceipt;

(b) shall be preserved by the Clerk for a period of two years from the date of filing, shall constitute part of the public records of his office, and shall be open to public inspection. (Aug. 2, 1946, c. 753, Title III, para. 306, 60 Stat. 841.)

266. Persons to whom applicable.—The provisions of this title |paras. 261-270 of this title| shall apply to any person (except a political committee as defined in the Federal Corrupt Practices Act, and duly organized State or local committees of a policial party), who by himself, or through any agent or employee or other persons in any manner whatsoever, directly or indirectly, solicits, collects, or receives money or any other thing of value to be used principally to aid, or the principal purpose of which person is to aid, in the accomplishment of any of the following purposes;

(a) The passage or defeat of any legislation by the Congress of the United States.

(b) To influence, directly or indirectly, the passage or defeat of any legislation by the Congress of the United States. (Aug. 2, 1946, c.

110

753, Title III, para. 307, 60 Stat. 841.)

267. Registration with Secretary of the Senate and Clerk of the House.— (a) Any person who shall engage himself for pay or for any consideration for the purpose of attempting to influence the passage or defeat of any legislation by the Congress of the United States shall, before doing anything in furtherance of such object, register with the Clerk of the House of Representatives and the Secretary of the Senate and shall give to those officers in writing and under oath, his name and business address, the name and address of the person by whom he is employed, and in whose interest he appears or works, the duration of such employment, how much he is paid and is to receive, by whom he is paid or is to be paid, how much he is to be paid for expenses, and what expenses are to be included. Each such person so registering shall, between the first and tenth day of each calendar quarter, so long as his activity continues, file with the Clerk and Secretary a detailed report under oath of all money received and expended by him during the preceding calendar quarter in carrying on his work; to whom paid; for what purposes; and the names of any papers, periodicals, magazines, or other publications in which he has caused to be published any articles or editorials, and the proposed legislation he is employed to support or oppose. The provisions of this section shall not apply to any person who merely appears before a committee of the Congress of the United States in support of or opposition to legislation; nor to any public official acting in his official capacity; nor in the case of any newspaper or other regularly published periodical (including any individual who owns, publishes, or is employed by any such newspaper or periodical) which in the ordinary course of business publishes news items, editorials, or other comments, or paid advertisements, which directly or indirectly urge the passage or defeat of legislation, if such newspaper, periodical, or individual, engages in no further or other activities in connection with the passage or defeat of such legislation, other than to appear before a committee of the Congress of the United States in support of or in opposition to such legislation.

(b) All information required to be filed under the provisions of this section with the Clerk of the House of Representatives and the Secretary of the Senate shall be compiled by said Clerk and Secretary, acting jointly, as soon as practicable after the close of the calendar quarter with respect to which such information is filed and shall be printed in the Congressional Record. (Aug. 2, 1946, c. 753, Title III, sec./ 308, 60 Stat. 841.)

*268. Reports and statements to be made under oath.—*All reports and statements required under this title (sec./ 261 and note-270 of this title) shall be made under oath, before an officer authorized by law to administer oaths. (Aug. 2, 1946, c. 753, Title III, sec./ 309, 60 Stat. 842.)

269. Penalties.—(a) Any person who violates any of the provisions of this title (sec./ 261 and note-270 of this title), shall, upon conviction, be guilty of a misdemeanor, and shall be punished by a fine of not more than $5,000 or imprisonment for not more than twelve months, or by both such fine and imprisonment.

(b) In addition to the penalties provided for in subsection (a), any person convicted of the misdemeanor specified therein is prohibited, for a period of three years from the date of such conviction, from attempting to influence, directly or indirectly, the passage or defeat of any pro posed legislation or from appearing before a committee of the Congress in support of or opposition to proposed legislation; and any person who violates any provision of this subsection shall, upon conviction thereof, be guilty of a felony, and shall be punished by a fine of not more than $10,000, or imprisonment for not more than five years, or by both such fine and imprisonment. (Aug. 2, 1946, c. 753, Title III, sec./ 310, 60 Stat. 842.)

270. Exemption.—The provisions of this title | sec./ 261 and note-270 of this title| shall not apply to practices or activities regulated by the Federal Corrupt Practices Act nor be construed as repealing any portion of said Federal Corrupt Practices Act. (Aug. 2, 1946, c. 753, Title III, sec./ 311, 60 Stat. 842.)

TITLE 5, U.S. CODE
POLITICAL ACTIVITY OF
CERTAIN STATE AND
LOCAL EMPLOYEES

Section 1501. Definitions.—For the purpose of this chapter | sec./ 1501-1508 of this title| —

(1) "State" means a State or territory or possession of the United States;

(2) "State or local agency" means the executive branch of a State, municipality, or other political subdivision of a State, or an agency or department thereof;

(3) "Federal agency" means an Executive agency or other agency of the United States, but does not include a member bank of the Federal Reserve System;

(4) "State or local officer or employee" means an individual employed by a State or local agency whose principal employment is in connection with an activity which is financed in whole or in part by loans or grants made by the United States or Federal agency, but does not

include—

(a) an individual who exercises no functions in connection with that activity; or

(b) an individual employed by an educational or research institution, establishment, agency, or system, which is supported in whole or in part by a State or political subdivision thereof, or by a recognized religious, philanthropic, or cultural organization; and

(5) the phrase "an active part in political management or in political campaigns" means those acts of political management or political campaigning which were prohibited on the part of employees in the competitive service before July 19, 1940, by determinations of the Civil Service Commission under the rules prescribed by the President. (Sept. 6, 1966, P. L. 89-554, sec./ 1, 80 Stat. 403.)

1502. Influencing elections—Taking part in political campaigns—Prohibitions—Exceptions.—(a) A State or local officer or employee may not—

(1) use his official authority or influence for the purpose of interfering with or affecting the result of an election or a nomination for office;

(2) directly or indirectly coerce, attempt to coerce, command, or advise a State or local officer or employee to pay, lend, or contribute anything of value to a party, committee, organization, agency, or person for political purposes; or

(3) take an active part in political management or in political campaigns.

(b) A State or local officer or employee retains the right to vote as he chooses and to express his opinions on political subjects and candidates.

(c) Subsection (a) (3) of this section does not apply to—

(1) the Governor or Lieutenant Governor of a State or an individual

authorized by law to act as Governor;

(2) the mayor of a city;

(3) a duly elected head of an executive department of a State or municipality who is not classified under a State or municipal merit or civil-service system; or;

(4) an individual holding elective office.

1503. Nonpartisan political activity permitted.—Section 1502 (a) (3) of this title does not prohibit political activity in connection with—

(1) an election and the preceding campaign if none of the candidates is to be nominated or elected at that election as representing a party any of whose candidates for presidential elector received votes in the last preceding election at which presidential electors were selected; or

(2) a question which is not specifically identified with a National or State political party.

For the purpose of this section, questions relating to constitutional amendments, referendums, approval of municipal ordinances, and others of a similar character, are deemed not specifically identified with a National or State political party. (Sept. 6, 1966, P. L. 89-554, sec./ 1, 80 Stat. 404.)

1504. Investigations — Notice of hearing.—When a Federal agency charged with the duty of making a loan or grant of funds of the United States for use in an activity by a State or local officer or employee has reason to believe that the officer or employee has violated section 1502 of this title, it shall report the matter to the Civil Service Commission. On receipt of the report, or on receipt of other information which seems to the Commission to warrant an investigation, the Commission shall—

(1) fix a time and place for a hearing; and

(2) send, by registered or certified mail, to the officer or employee charged with the violation and to the State or local agency employing him a notice setting forth a summary of the alleged violation and giving the time and place of the hearing.

The hearing may not be held earlier than 10 days after the mailing of the notice. (Sept. 6, 1966, P. L. 89-554, sec./ 1, 80 Stat. 405.)

1505. Hearings — Adjudications —Notice of determinations.—Either the State or local officer or employee or the State or local agency employing him, or both, are entitled to appear with counsel at the hearing under section 1504 of this title, and be heard. After this hearing, the Civil Service Commission shall—

(1) determine whether a violation of section 1502 of this title has occurred;

(2) determine whether the violation warrants the removal of the officer or employee from his office or employment; and

(3) notify the officer or employee and the agency of the determination by registered or certified mail. (Sept. 6, 1966, P. L. 89-554, sec./ 1, 80 Stat. 405.)

1506. Orders — Witholding loans or grants — Limitations. — (a) When the Civil Service Commission finds—

(1) that a State or local officer or employee has not been removed from his office or employment within 30 days after notice of a determination by the Commission that he has violated section 1502 of this title and that the violation warrants removal; or

(2) that the State or local officer or employee has been removed and has been appointed within 18 months after his removal to an office or employment in the same State in a State or local agency which does not receive loans or grants from a Federal agency; the Commission shall

make and certify to the appropriate Federal agency an order requiring that agency to withhold from its loans or grants to the State or local agency to which notice was given an amount equal to 2 years' pay at the rate the officer or employee was receiving at the time of the violation. When the State or local agency to which appointment within 18 months after removal has been made is one that receives loans or grants from a Federal agency, the Commission order shall direct that the withholding be made from that State or local agency.

(b) Notice of the order shall be sent by registered or certified mail to the State or local agency from which the amount is ordered to be withheld. After the order becomes final, the Federal agency to which the order is certified shall withhold the amount in accordance with the terms of the order. Except as provided by section 1508 of this title, a determination or order of the Commission becomes final at the end of 30 days after mailing the notice of the determination or order.

(c) The Commission may not require an amount to be withheld from a loan or grant pledged by a State or local agency as security for its bonds or notes if the withholding of that amount would jeopardize the payment of the principal or interest on the bonds or notes. (Sept. 6, 1966, P. L. 89-554, sec./ 1, 80 Stat. 405.)

1507. Subpenas and depositions— (a) The Civil Service Commission may require by subpena the attendance and testimony of witnesses and the production of documentary evidence relating to any matter before it as a result of this chapter (sec./ 1501-1508 of this title). Any member of the Commission may sign subpenas, and members of the Commission and its examiners when authorized by the Commission may administer oaths, examine witnesses, and

receive evidence. The attendance of witnesses and the production of documentary evidence may be required from any place in the United States at the designated place of hearing. In case of disobedience to a subpena, the Commission may invoke the aid of a court of the United States in requiring the attendance and testimony of witnesses and the production of documentary evidence. In case of contumacy or refusal to obey a subpena issued to a person, the United States District Court within whose jurisdiction the inquiry is carried on may issue an order requiring him to appear before the Commission, or to produce documentary evidence if so ordered, or to give evidence concerning the matter in question; and any failure to obey the order of the court may be punished by the court as a contempt thereof.

(b) The Commission may order testimony to be taken by deposition at any stage of a proceeding or investigation before it as a result of this chapter (sec./ 1501-1508 of this title). Depositions may be taken before an individual designated by the Commission and having the power to administer oaths. Testimony shall be reduced to writing by the individual taking the deposition, or under his direction, and shall be subscribed by the deponent. Any person may be compelled to appear and depose and to produce documentary evidence before the Commission as provided by this section.

(c) A person may not be excused from attending and testifying or from producing documentary evidence or in obedience to a subpena on the ground that the testimony or evidence, documentary or otherwise, required of him may tend to incriminate him or subject him to a penalty or forfeiture for or on account of any transaction, matter, or thing concerning which he is compelled to testify, or produce evidence, documentary or otherwise, before the

Commission in obedience to a subpena issued by it. A person so testifying is not exempt from prosecution and punishment for perjury committed in so testifying. (Sept. 6, 1966, P. L. 89-554, sec./ 1, 80 Stat. 406.)

1508. Judicial review.—A party aggrieved by a determination or order of the Civil Service Commission under section 1504, 1505, or 1506 of this title may, within 30 days after the mailing of notice of the determination or order, institute proceedings for review thereof by filing a petition in the United States District Court for the district in which the State or local officer or employee resides. The institution of the proceedings does not operate as a stay of the determination or order unless—

(1) the court specifically orders a stay; and

(2) the officer or employee is suspended from his office or employment while the proceedings are pending.

A copy of the petition shall immediately be served on the Commission, and thereupon the Commission shall certify and file in the court a transcript of the record on which the determination or order was made. The court shall review the entire record including questions of fact and questions of law. If application is made to the court for leave to adduce additional evidence, and it is shown to the satisfaction of the court that the additional evidence may materially affect the result of the proceedings and that there were reasonable grounds for failing to adduce this evidence in the hearing before the Commission, the court may direct that the additional evidence may be taken before the Commission in the manner and on the terms and conditions fixed by the court. The Commission may modify its findings of fact or its determination or order in view of the additional evidence and shall file with the court the modified findings, determination or order; and the modified findings of fact, if supported by substantial evidence, are conclusive. The court shall affirm the determination or or order, of the modified determination or order, if the court determines that it is in accordance with law. If the court determines that the determination or order, or the modified determination or order, is not in accordance with law, the court shall remand the proceeding to the Commission with directions either to make a determination or order determined by the court to be lawful or to take such further proceedings, as, in the opinion of the court, the law requires. The judgment and decree of the court are final, subject to review by the appropriate United States Court of Appeals as in other cases, and the judgment and decree of the court of appeals are final, subject to review by the Supreme Court of the United States on certiorari or certification as provided by section 1254 of title 28. If a provision of this section is held to be invalid as applied to a party by a determination or order of the Commission, the determination or order becomes final and effective as to that party as if the provision had not been enacted. (Sept. 6, 1966, P. L. 89-554, sec./ 1, 80 Stat. 406.)

POLITICAL ACTIVITIES

7321. Political contributions and services.—The President may prescribe rules which shall provide, as nearly as conditions of good administration warrant, that an employee in an Executive agency or in the competitive service is not obliged, by reason of that employment, to contribute to a political fund or to render political service, and that he may not be removed or otherwise prejudiced for refusal to do so. (Sept. 6, 1966, P. L. 89-554, sec./ 1, 80 Stat. 525.)

7322. *Political use of authority or influence — Prohibition.*—The President may prescribe rules which shall provide, as nearly as conditions of good administration warrant, that an employee in an Executive agency or in the competitive service may not use his official authority or influence to coerce the political action of a person or body. (Sept. 6, 1966, P. L. 89-554, sec./ 1, 80 Stat. 525.)

7323. *Political contributions—Prohibition.*—An employee in an Executive agency (except one appointed by the President, by and with the advice and consent of the Senate) may not request or receive from, or give to, an employee, a Member of Congress, or an officer of a uniformed service a thing of value for political purposes. An employee who violates this section shall be removed from the service. (Sept. 6, 1966, P. L. 89-554, sec./ 1, 80 Stat. 525.)

7324. *Influencing elections — Taking part in political campaigns — Prohibitions — Exceptions.* —(a) An employee in an Executive agency or an individual employed by the government of the District of Columbia may not—

(1) use his official authority or influence for the purpose of interfering with or affecting the result of an election; or

(2) take an active part in political management or in political campaigns.

For the purpose of this subsection, the phrase "an active part in political management or in political campaigns" means those acts of political management or political campaigning which were prohibited on the part of employees in the competitive service before July 19, 1940, by determinations of the Civil Service Commission under the rules prescribed by the President.

(b) An employee or individual to whom subsection (a) of this section applies retains the right to vote as he chooses and to express his opinion on political subjects and candidates.

(c) Subsection (a) of this section does not apply to an individual employed by an educational or research institution, establishment, agency, or system which is supported in whole or in part by the District of Columbia or by a recognized religious, philanthropic, or cultural organization.

(d) Subsection (a) (2) of this section does not apply to—

(1) an employee paid from the appropriation for the office of the President;

(2) the head or the assistant head of an Executive department or military department;

(3) an employee appointed by the President, by and with the advice and consent of the Senate, who determines policies to be pursued by the United States in its relations with foreign powers or in the nationwide administration of Federal laws.

(4) the Commissioners of the District of Columbia; or

(5) the Recorder of Deeds of the District of Columbia, (Sept. 6, 1966, P. L. 89-554, sec./ 1, 80 Stat. 525.)

7325. *Penalties.*—An employee or individual who violates section 7324 of this title shall be removed from his position, and funds appropriated for the position from which removed thereafter may not be used to pay the employee or individual. However, if the Civil Service Commission finds by unanimous vote that the violation does not warrant removal, a penalty of not less than 30 days' suspension without pay shall be imposed by direction of the Commission. (Sept. 6, 1966, P. L. 89-554, sec./ 1, 80 Stat. 526.)

7326. *Nonpartisan political activity permitted.*—Section 7324 (a) (2) of this title does not prohibit political activity in connection with—

(1) an election and the preceding campaign if none of the candidates is to be nominated or elected at that election as representing a party any of whose candidates for presidential elector received votes in the last preceding election at which presidential electors were selected; or

(2) a question which is not specifically identified with a National or State political party or political party of a territory or possession of the United States.

For the purpose of this section, questions relating to constitutional amendments, referendums, approval of municipal ordinances, and others of a similar character, are deemed not specifically identified with a National or State political party or political party of a territory or possession of the United States. (Sept. 6, 1966, P. L. 89-554, sec./ 1, 80 Stat. 526.)

7327. *Political activity permitted — Employees residing in certain municipalities.*—(a) Section 7324 (a) (2) of this title does not apply to an employee of The Alaska Railroad who resides in a municipality on the line of the railroad in respect to political activities involving that municipality.

(b) The Civil Service Commission may prescribe regulations permitting employees and individuals to whom section 7324 of this title applies to take an active part in political management and political campaigns involving the municipality or other political subdivision in which they reside, to the extent the Commission considers it to be in their domestic interest, when—

(1) the municipality or political subdivision is in Maryland or Virginia and in the immediate vicinity of the District of Columbia, or is a municipality in which the majority of voters are employed by the Government of the United States; and

(2) the Commission determines that because of special or unusual circumstances which exist in the municipality or political subdivision it is in the domestic interest of the employees and individuals to permit that political participation. (Sept. 6, 1966, P. L. 89-554, sec./ 1, 80 Stat. 526.)

INDEX

LEGAL ALMANAC SERIES

LAW FOR THE LAYMAN • COVERS ALL STATES

Price Per Volume: $3.00, $3.50 for No. 9

Oceana Publications, Inc.

75 Main Street   **Dobbs Ferry, N.Y. 10522**